EXCEPTIONAL TEACHING

A Comprehensive Guide for Including **Students With Disabilities**

JIM PIERSON

T. THOMPSON

Standard PUBLISHING
CINCINNATI, OHIO

DEDICATION

To my wife, Norma,
my best friend, my most trusted adviser, and my constant encourager

With gratefulness, I acknowledge

The inspiration and ideas I have gained from the many Sunday schoolteachers
and children's pastors I have met at conferences, churches, and seminars who
have included students with disabilities in their classes and programs

The expectations of my students in special education and disability ministry
who wanted me to give them quality information and guidance

The joy that comes from the successful inclusion experiences
of many people with disabilities

The appreciation of families whose children were included with their peers

The hard work of Judy Davis, Rachel Pierson, and Carolyn Proctor, who deciphered my handwriting, processed the words, and kept my computer going

The professionalism and encouragement of my editor, Theresa Hayes

Standard Publishing, Cincinnati, Ohio 45231
A division of Standex International Corporation
© 2002 by Jim Pierson. All rights reserved.
Printed in the United States of America

09 08 07 06 05 04 03 02   9 8 7 6 5 4 3 2 1

Library of Congress Cataloging-in-Publication Data
Pierson, Jim (O.)
    Exceptional teaching : a comprehensive guide for including students with disabilities/
Jim Pierson.
        p.cm.
    Includes bibliographical references (p.) and index.
    ISBN 0-7847-1255-7
Handicapped children—Education—United States—Handbooks, manuals, etc. 2.
Christian education of handicapped children—United States—Handbooks, manuals, etc. 3.
Inclusive education—United States—Handbooks, manuals, etc. I. Title.

LC4031 .P49 2002
371.9'0973—dc21   2001049758

Permission is granted to reproduce material from this book for ministry purposes only.

All Scripture quotations, unless otherwise indicated, are taken from the HOLY BIBLE, NEW INTERNATIONAL VERSION®.
NIV®. Copyright © 1973, 1978, 1984 by International Bible Society. Used by permission of Zondervan Publishing House. All
rights reserved.

Edited by Theresa C. Hayes
Cover design Ewa Pol

Table of Contents

Introduction

The primary aim of this book is to give you the information you need to be able to help a student with a disability and/or special needs feel comfortable and included in your classroom.

The book contains
▼ information that will give you basic facts about a given disability or disorder;
▼ information that will enable you to create a positive learning environment for the student with the disability;
▼ information that will aid the learning process for the student.

The public school system uses a somewhat uniform list of eighteen categories of students with disabilities. I have used that list to organize this book. "Hearing Impaired" and "Deaf" and "Visually Impaired" and "Blind" have been blended for convenience. Special attention will be given to the most common diagnosis within a category.

In order to receive special education services, the student must have documentation that he or she fits in one of the categories listed below.

1. Learning Disabled
2. Mentally Retarded
3. Gifted
4. Speech Impaired
5. Language Impaired
6. Emotionally Disturbed
7. Autism
8. Health Impaired
9. Physically Impaired
10. Hearing Impaired
11. or Deaf
12. Visually Impaired
13. or Blind
14. Deaf-Blind
15. Multidisabled
16. Functionally Delayed
17. Developmentally Delayed
18. Traumatic Brain Injury

Following the descriptions of each of these disabilities, you will find steps for developing a program in your school, unique suggestions for helping the family, a list of resources, and some good programs to examine. Any resource that I consider "a must see" will be listed with the specific diagnosis. Additional material of value will be listed in the resource section.

To solve the editorial problem of the pronoun gender, "he" or "she," I will use the gender that is favored by the disability. In most cases, it will be "he."

Disability happens more often to boys than it does to girls. To date there is only one diagnosis that affects girls only, and that is Rett syndrome.

I have compiled the material in this book from
▼ projects of my college students
▼ churches with successful programs
▼ children's and disability ministers who are experts in an area
▼ other books I have written
▼ ideas I have gained from participating in workshops and seminars
▼ packets of material provided by Christian Church Foundation for the
    Handicapped
▼ materials in my files
▼ books I like
▼ disability ministry directors who have developed useful materials.

Since this book caught your eye, you don't need to be convinced of the need to provide Christian education for students with special needs. Therefore, my primary purpose is not to motivate, but to inform. I have assumed that the reader of this book is a frontline worker. While writing, I would often ask myself, "How would I say this if I were standing in the classroom with the teacher?" My prayer is that in this book you will find a friend who wants to help you.

How we got to this point

Students with disabilities are showing up more frequently in Christian education programs. While we welcome them, their presence can present some concern for the teacher who feels that he or she doesn't have the skills to teach the student. These fears can be relieved by some basic information. That basic information is the focus of this book.

Let's talk a bit about how we arrived at this point. In 1975, Congress passed a mandatory education law that requires the school system to provide a free and appropriate education for every child in its jurisdiction who has a defined disability. A part of the law was the "least restrictive environment" (LRE) concept. In short, the student was to be educated in the classroom with his peers. LRE led to mainstreaming, mainstreaming led to inclusion, and inclusion led to full inclusion. Because parents are accustomed to having their children in inclusive programs in the school system, they rightly expect that inclusion is available in their church's education unit.

The idea of inclusion has been enhanced in the general community by other laws and organizations. The Americans With Disabilities Act (ADA), passed in 1990, says that people with disabilities should be able to move easily in their

Jim Pierson's prayer is that

in this book you will find

a friend who wants to help you.

communities by having access to transportation, communication, and employment. The Special Olympics, organized in 1963, has provided visible evidence that people with disabilities are among us and want to be a part of our world. Television advertisements frequently employ people with disabilities, as in the example of the mother who purchases a particular washing detergent in order to have more valuable time with her daughter who has Down syndrome.

Inclusion is a concept that should be embraced by Christians. If possible, the student with a disability should be included in the classroom with his age-mates. If there are enough students with a similar diagnosis, say mental retardation or learning disabilities, then putting the students together for the lesson period would be fine. However, it is important that these students be able to interact with others in the class. Sometimes, for a variety of reasons, parents of children with disabilities may not want their child included. Initially, their request should be respected, but they should be helped to understand that the goal is eventual full inclusion for their child.

The religious community recognizes the importance of providing spiritual nurture for its members with disabilities. Faith groups hire consultants in special education to work with their congregations in including the disability community. Christian publishers develop materials for use in the Christian education of persons with disabilities. Disability ministry is becoming a profession all its own. But the best motivation for including the learner with a disability in a Christian education program is two thousand years old. Jesus instructed His followers to "Go into all the world and preach the good news to all creation" (Mark 16:15). "All creation" makes the directive inclusive. There is no footnote. Age, intelligence, physical ability, emotional level, visual acuity, and other people separators are not restrictions to the projected recipients of the gospel.

What did Jesus do?
Including students with disabilities is often seen as an overwhelming, seemingly impossible task. Instead of dwelling on the thousands of people who have a given disability, focus on one individual who has it. Teachers need to use Jesus' mathematics—leave the ninety-nine to instruct the one. A description of an event

from Jesus' life suggests this concept. Recognizing His concern for them, people with disabilities came to Him in droves: "Jesus . . . went up on a mountainside and sat down. Great crowds came to him, bringing the lame, the blind, the crippled, the mute and many others, and laid them at his feet; and he healed them" (Matthew 15:29, 30). The fact that He was seated suggests that He dealt with each case individually, not the whole crowd at the same time.

I imagine a young husband and wife approaching the seated Includer. She carries a six-month-old girl who was born without vision. The child's father asks, "Will You make our daughter see?"

Jesus reaches for the baby and asks, "What is her name?"

"Rebekah," says her mother as she gently places the baby in His arms.

"Do you have other children?"

"No," sighs the mother.

Jesus turns to the father, "What is your trade?"

"I am a carpenter."

Jesus smiles. "I learned that trade." He pulls the blanket away from the baby's face, touches His finger to His tongue, and touches her eyes, asking God to open her eyes. The father and mother hold each other tightly. Jesus smiles.

While we cannot heal the physical infirmities of our students with a touch, we can touch them in a loving manner. As you would with any student, always respect an individual's personal space, but don't be afraid to touch a person with a disability. A warm handclasp or a hand on the shoulder can convey volumes about your acceptance of and love for the person. Some children, as will be noted later, have a great aversion to being touched. In those cases, you will show your respect for the child through whatever touch and eye contact they are comfortable with, kind speech, and warm smiles.

Jesus' methods reflect notable inclusion principles. First, He involved the person with the disability in the ministry process. He didn't discuss the case with a committee, or even launch a plan of His own. He asked what the person wanted. Jesus asked a man with a physical disability if he wanted to be healed (John 5:6) and a man who was blind what he wanted Him to do for him (Mark 10:51). He involved the person in the ministry plan!

Jesus' approach suggests that the focus of ministry should be *with* the person, not *to*. The teacher should ask the family of the student in her class what they want for the child. Work out goals for the student to learn about Jesus.

A second principle our Lord models is a quick, personal, and thorough response to need. Luke noted that Jesus stopped in mid-step when He heard a man who was blind call for help (Luke 18:38-40). When the man with leprosy felt Jesus' touch, he knew real inclusion (Luke 5:12-14). When Jesus healed the blind man and the healing was incomplete, Jesus stayed with him until he could see. He repeated the process. He was involved! (Mark 8:22-26). Jesus' example is a good one for us. Yes, you may need additional helpers in the room in order to be able to pay such personal attention to those who need it. There are those in every congregation who may not have the gift of teaching, but who nevertheless love children. Becoming a teacher's aide, or personal friend to the student with a disability, is a perfect ministry for them. (See "Exceptional Teaching Tips" on page eighteen.)

Jesus believed that helping people was more important than arbitrary rules and regulations. Telling a man who was paralyzed, "Pick up your mat and walk," brought down the wrath of the Pharisees. It was not right, they said, to carry a mat on the Sabbath! You will likewise encounter those who say to you, "But we've never needed to teach like this before!" Be prepared to respond kindly to them, explaining the needs of these special students. Help them to understand that people are more important than methods or tradition.

Another of Jesus' inclusive ministry principles was sensitivity to the family of the person with a disability. Jesus healed a boy with epilepsy after His disciples couldn't (Mark 9:20-24). He then radiated a warm concern for the boy's parents. He asked, "How long has he been like this?"

The father replied, "From childhood. [The spirit] has often thrown him into fire or water to kill him." Jesus' question, and His attention to the answer, is exemplary. Expressing interest in the person and his family is far better than a stare or a turned head. Be prepared and be willing to spend some time listening. Parents of children with disabilities often need the ministry of a patient listener!

Sometimes parents are blamed for the disability of a child. Such an approach did not originate with Jesus. After meeting a man who was born blind, Jesus' disciples revealed their judgmental thoughts (John 9:1-3). Their exchange and Jesus' response provide an eternal answer to the reason for a disability. The man's condition was not due to either his sin or that of his parents. His blindness happened, Jesus said, "So that the work of God might be displayed in his life" (John 9:3). There is no reason to blame, but every reason to support the family, and to display God's mercy, kindness, love, and hope in the lives of the child and his parents.

Jesus was an includer. When responding to people with disabilities, His unconditional love was obvious. Allowing His kind of love to work in our hearts will insure the inclusion of persons with disabilities in our classrooms.

CHAPTER 1

Students With
LEARNING
DISABILITIES

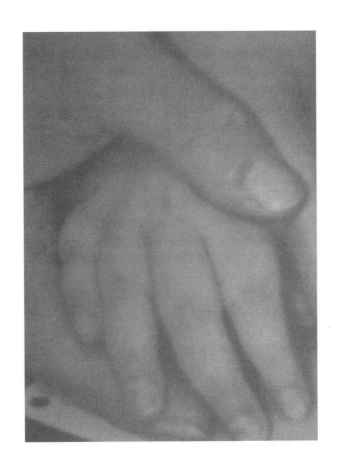

A learning disability is a disorder that

▼ Affects the student's ability to interpret what he sees or hears.

▼ Interferes with the ability to integrate information from the various parts of his brain.

▼ Results in difficulties in speech and language, attention, self-control, and coordination.

Because students with learning disabilities make up the largest disability group served by special education in America (more than 50 percent), it is very likely that they will attend your class.

If I had a learning disability, here is what I would want my teacher to know about me:

▼ I am trying to sit still.

▼ I can't keep my mind on one subject very long.

▼ A noise outside will distract me.

▼ I don't always pick up on cues about how you are feeling.

▼ I can be impulsive. Often I do something and then think about it.

▼ I try to listen, but my mind wanders.

▼ I don't always remember.

▼ I lose my belongings.

▼ In my mind, one and one do not always equal two.

▼ Often I feel stupid.

▼ I am really a nice person trying to learn and stay focused.

▼ I get frustrated.

Let's understand the definition of the Individuals With Disabilities Education Act (IDEA). It had its beginning in 1975 as "PL-94-142" (named the "Education of All Handicapped Students Act"). It was most recently amended in 1997 and is now

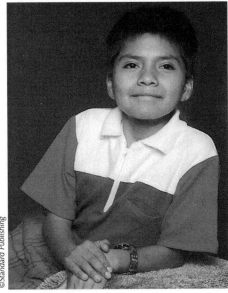

©Standard Publishing

Renato's learning disabilities don't do much to dampen his spirit or diminish his personality. Renato, like any boy his age, requires a firm, patient, and loving teacher.

"PL-105-17." I have used IDEA's definition of various categories of children with disabilities throughout this book. If you are interested in a more detailed look at the law, check with the U.S. Department of Education at 800-USA-LEARN, or at http://www.ed.gov.index.html. IDEA says that a learning disability is "a disorder in one or more of the basic psychological processes involved in understanding or using language, spoken or written, which disorder may manifest itself in an imperfect ability to listen, think, speak, read, write, spell, or do mathematical calculations. The term includes such conditions as perceptual disabilities, brain injury, minimal brain dysfunction, dyslexia, and developmental aphasia. The term does not include a learning problem that is primarily the result of visual, hearing, or motor disabilities, of mental retardation, of emotional disturbance, or of environmental, cultural or economic disadvantage."

Three factors emerge from this definition:
▼ The student with a learning disability will have a normal or above normal IQ.
▼ He will have a specific behavior and/or learning problem.
▼ The cause of the learning disability is likely neurological.

Learning disabilities can be divided into three broad categories:
▼ **Developmental speech and language disorders** (It is noteworthy that often the first indicator of a learning problem is a speech or language problem.)
   – Developmental articulation disorder
   – Developmental expressive language disorder
   – Developmental receptive language disorder

▼ **Academic skills disorders**
   – Developmental reading disorder (dyslexia) (Reading disorders account for 80 percent of learning disabilities.)
   – Developmental writing disorder (handwriting, spelling, and written expression)
   – Developmental arithmetic disorder

▼ **Attention deficit disorders**
   – ADD means attention deficit disorder.
   – ADHD means attention deficit hyperactivity disorder

The terms ADD and ADHD are common in the education world. Since the abilities to pay attention to the material being presented, and to sit still are so critical to good learning, the teacher needs to be aware of students with ADD and ADHD.

Sometimes students with ADD and ADHD are discussed as though they are not in the learning disability category. Medically, that is probably correct. However, the basic similarity between a student with a learning disability and a student with ADD or ADHD is simple. Neither can pay attention to a task and both exhibit a lot of meaningless movement. If the student has ADD, he is less hyperactive and impulsive. The diagnostic criteria for ADD and ADHD are in the

Diagnostic and Statistical Manual of Mental Disorders (DSM-IV). The DSM outlines the symptoms of inattention, hyperactivity, and impulsiveness the child demonstrates in two settings (say school and home) by the time he is seven. These symptoms are not a part of any other disorder or problem.

"Dyslexia" is often used when describing a child with a learning disability. Dyslexia, however, is a specific term to denote that the child has difficulty reading. If a parent uses the term, ask if the disability is broader than reading.

"Dyscalculia" means that the child has trouble with mathematics.

"Dysgraphia" means that he has difficulty with writing.

In all cases of a child with a learning disability, there are problems stemming from the child's inability to focus. The suggestions in this section will assist you in including these students in your classroom.

Characteristics of students with learning disabilities

▼ attention deficits
▼ hyperactivity
▼ memory deficits
▼ perceptual deficits
▼ cognitive deficits
▼ motor and coordination difficulties (fine and gross skills are often poor)
▼ general orientation (may have trouble distinguishing between left and right)
▼ emotional liability (may cry when laughing is more appropriate)
▼ may be immature for his age

As a result, the teacher will note that the child

▼ has difficulty sitting still, moves around a lot
▼ touches the wall or the student next to him
▼ doesn't read well
▼ doesn't write well
▼ jumps to conclusions
▼ doesn't remember what he is told to do
▼ can't wait his turn
▼ changes from one uncompleted task to another
▼ confuses and misunderstands directions
▼ is awkward/clumsy
▼ has a low tolerance for frustration
▼ relates poorly in a group
▼ is immature for his age
▼ interrupts frequently
▼ laughs inappropriately
▼ annoys other students
▼ talks to self while working
▼ has a limited vocabulary
▼ has difficulty expressing wants
▼ has low self-esteem

Create a Welcoming Environment By

▼ keeping classroom noise to a minimum

▼ teaching students to use some basic gestures

▼ assisting with small hand activities such as pasting and using scissors

▼ allowing enough space for pictures to be larger

▼ not distributing materials until you are ready for them to be used

▼ using lots of visual and other sensory materials (Use each of the senses at least once per lesson.)

▼ keeping directions simple and deliver them one at a time

▼ posting the rules in the classroom

▼ showing love and concern with discipline you mete

▼ using an easy to understand and read version of the Scriptures (See the resource section for suggestions.)

▼ varying the activities

▼ encouraging students to use a ruler when reading

▼ reading all written directions aloud

▼ using role play to practice problem solving

▼ teaching memory work with lots of clues and cues

▼ avoiding "round-robin" reading

▼ praising every student, but looking for ways to praise the student with LD

▼ being sure the student is listening

▼ changing the pace and activities in the classroom frequently

▼ making every member of the class feel competent

▼ creating an atmosphere of tolerance and acceptance

▼ using lots of repetition

Medicating students with learning disabilities

Medications can effectively control impulsiveness and other symptoms of hyper-active disorders, improve the student's attention span, and help him focus. Students with ADHD seem to get the most benefit from medications. Medications get the best results when the physician is working with the parents to adjust the correct amount. Some 90 percent of students with hyperactivity can be helped by medication.

Tell parents that you are not able to medicate a child in your classroom. Medical and legal restraints justify your decision. Your role is teacher, not nurse. If the child's medication must be administered during your class time, ask the parent to come and give it. If the medication the student is taking seems to interfere with his responsiveness, you may want to know what he is taking. While you could find out about the possible side effects of a specific medicine, this knowledge will not assist you in teaching the student.

If you notice behaviors that you believe are caused by the medication, report your observations to the parent. In all likelihood, the doctor has asked the family to let him know the student's reactions to the medicine. Knowing such details helps to regulate the dosage and to know if another medicine would be more helpful.

Blaming the parents

"If his parents would make him mind, that child wouldn't have learning disabili-ties" is a frequently heard judgment. The fact is that neurological problems cause learning disabilities, not poor parenting. Find ways to encourage the family instead of ways to blame them.

©2001 Jim West

Students with learning disabilities will have nomal or above normal IQs. However, the disorder affects their ability to interpret what they see and hear.

Exceptional Teaching Tips

▼ Unless there are several students with learning problems in the same general age range, place the student in the class with his peers. If there are several, arrange for them to be with their non-disabled friends for group activities.

▼ **Train a volunteer to be a buddy.**
   – For very young children, adults work well.
   – For elementary-age children, high school students are excellent.
   – For junior and senior high age groups, same-age peer advocates tend to be most helpful. Train the members of the class how to help their peer.
   – Assigning a buddy to the student is particularly helpful until he adjusts to the routine of the class.
   – Provide one-on-one help for fine motor tasks such as cutting.

▼ **Seek advice and information from the people who know the child best.** Ask the family if there are professionals in their child's life who have helpful information to offer. If so, have them give the appropriate permission for you to communicate with the professional. You certainly will want to talk to the child's schoolteacher. Getting information about the child from a person in another educational setting will be invaluable to you.

▼ **Set reasonable goals for your special learner. Goals like**
   – understanding his personal value and worth as a child of God
   – understanding God's love and His plan for salvation
   – taking responsibility for his decisions and choices
   – developing competency in social skills
   – developing communication skills
   – developing friendships

▼ **Work on goals that are particularly important in a Christian environment:**
   – understanding that God's love is unconditional
   – developing a positive self-concept
   – making good choices
   – being responsible

▼ **Provide purposeful movement**—teach gestures or sign language to the child to accompany what is being learned.

▼ **Provide necessary breaks in concentration.**

▼ **Offer helpful classroom supplies,** such as two-handed scissors, jumbo crayons, and pencil grips.

As you work with the student, you will be able to add your own tips to this list.

CHAPTER 2

Students With
MENTAL RETARDATION

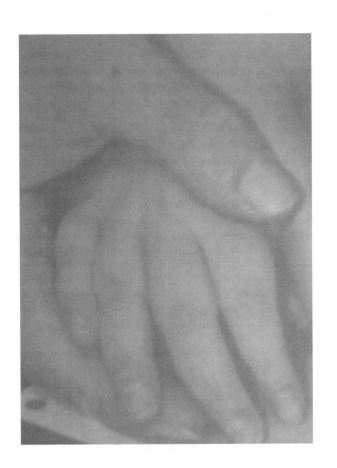

An Exceptional Life Story

Amanda is four years old. Her red hair and ready smile gain positive attention. An observer will note that she walks more like a two-year-old and her speech consists mainly of one-word responses. She looks like the other students in the room with her. The difference is that she is behind in reaching her developmental milestones. She walked late, she talked late, and she is not toilet trained. While her mother reports that the pregnancy was without incident, Amanda suffered anoxia (the lack of oxygen) during the birth process. The oxygen deprivation caused mental retardation.

Mental retardation happens to a real child who has a name. In his developmental history he didn't get enough oxygen, got an extra or frayed chromosome, suffered a blow to the head, or something else happened. He is not like another student with mental retardation. His attitude, personality, and approach to life differ as much as those of a student without mental retardation.

Some helpful information about MR:

Having some basic information about mental retardation will help you understand a student like Amanda in your classroom.

▼ It is not a disease. It cannot be caught.
▼ It is not mental illness.
▼ It is permanent. The child will not grow out of it.

In a nutshell, having mental retardation means that something happened to interfere with the development of the brain. As the child grew, the information coming from his senses was not processed and integrated in his brain. As a result, he doesn't have as much information as his peers and will always obtain it more slowly than his peers.

The student with mental retardation has the capacity to learn, to develop, and to grow. He can make a positive impact on his family, community, and your class.

If the student in your class has a label of mental retardation, it means three factors have been considered. First, the student has an Intellectual Quotient of less than seventy. Second, he will not adapt to his surroundings well. His speech and language skills, his self-care routines, his social interactions, his self-direction, his use of his community, and his ability to work will not match those of his age-mates without mental retardation. Third, whatever caused his mental retardation happened before his eighteenth birthday. The last factor is probably the most important to his being in your classroom. Whatever happened, happened early. That is the significance of mental retardation's being a developmental disorder.

Definitions

The Individuals With Disabilities Education Act (IDEA, 1997) defines mental retardation as follows: "Mental retardation means significantly subaverage general intellectual functioning existing concurrently with deficits in adaptive behavior and manifested during the developmental period that adversely affects a student's educational performance."

The American Association on Mental Retardation (1992) defines mental retardation as: "Mental retardation refers to substantial limitations in present functioning. It is characterized by significantly subaverage intellectual functioning, existing concurrently with related limitations in two or more of the following applicable adaptive skill areas: communication, self-care, home living, social skills, community use, self-direction, health and safety, functional academics, leisure, and work. Mental retardation manifests before age eighteen."

Causes of mental retardation

There are many causes of mental retardation. The most important thing for you, the teacher, to remember is that the student in your classroom could not help what happened to him; the cause was out of his control.

The causes are first categorized into three groups of times when the retardation occurs, and then categorized into six subgroups:

▼ **Prenatal** (before birth)
  – Genetic: When genes from Mom and Dad combine, errors can occur. More than five hundred genetic diseases are associated with mental retardation. Down syndrome is the most familiar genetic disorder.
  – Malnutrition during pregnancy, toxoplasmosis, smoking, drinking alcohol, taking drugs, and being HIV infected are some of the factors that can damage the child.
  – One or more abortions in the mother's past, especially dilation and extraction abortion in the second trimester. According to the article, "Detrimental Effects of Adolescent Abortion," written by Amy R. Sobie and Dr. David C. Reardon, published in the January/March 2001 issue of *The Post-Abortion Review*, these abortions are associated with low birth weight in later pregnancies, which can cause various health and developmental problems for the baby, including cerebral palsy. One cause of premature birth of subsequent babies is the spontaneous dilation of the cervix because the cervix has been artificially dilated several times before this pregnancy. (For more on this issue, see the resource section.)

▼ **Perinatal** (during birth)
  – Anoxia (oxygen deprivation), caused by the position of the umbilical cord, a breech birth, low birth weight, and a premature birth can all result in mental retardation.

▼ **Postnatal** (after birth)
   – Childhood diseases, such as meningitis and encephalitis, accidents, (such as a near drowning or a blow to the head), can damage the brain. Sadly, child abuse is an ever-growing cause of postnatal damage to the brain. For more on this topic, see pages 69-70, 169-170.
   – Environmental: Toxins (such as lead and mercury), poverty, malnutrition, poor medical care, and an environment lacking stimulation can lead to irreversible damage resulting in mental retardation.

Prevention of mental retardation

The number of cases of mental retardation would decrease if we worked harder to improve, change, modify, or otherwise do something about the following:

▼ injuries resulting from vehicular accidents
▼ poor or no prenatal care
▼ child abuse and neglect
▼ environmental toxins
▼ low birth weight
▼ teen pregnancy
▼ poor nutrition
▼ sexually transmitted diseases
▼ lack of early assistance
▼ abortion

Are you surprised to see the last item on that list? You could not be faulted for never having heard before that abortion may lead to disabilities in subsequent children, because the mainstream media certainly isn't interested in disseminating this information. Brent Rooney wrote an article titled, "Is Cerebral Palsy Ever a 'Choice'?" that was published in the October/December 2000 issue of *The Post-Abortion Review*. In this article, Rooney states that "At least sixteen studies, including one published in the prestigious *New England Journal of Medicine*, support the claim that a previous induced abortion elevates the subsequent risk of a premature birth.

"Most recently, a study of more than 61,000 Danish women, the largest study ever on premature births, found that women with previous induced abortions had double the risk of very preterm births (births before thirty-four weeks gestation) and almost double the risk of preterm births compared to women with no history of abortion. Women who had two previous 'evacuation' type abortions had a twelve times higher risk of prematurity compared to women who had not had abortions."

And, as I have noted earlier in this book, premature babies run a whole gamut of mental and physical development risks. Rooney's article goes on to calculate the number of newborns with CP born to moms who had prior induced abortions.

General factors influencing learning

Having a limited intelligence causes the learner to have some problems the teacher will want to work to remedy.

▼ Help the student focus his **attention**.

▼ Heighten the student's **memory skills**, especially the short-term ones.

▼ Help the student **generalize** the information he learns from one area to another. For example, help him transfer skills he learns in your classroom to the weekday program he is in, or to the playground.

▼ Constant failure will erode the student's **motivation**. Do everything to look for one (small though it be) area of success and accent it. Be his cheerleader.

Adaptive behaviors

The student's limited ability to adapt to his environment can be improved if the teacher understands his limitations. The following ten areas of adaptive skills can provide a springboard for the teacher to help a student who has mental retardation:

▼ **Communication** (listening, understanding, gesturing, speaking, reading, writing, moving, all of the elements of relating to communicating with another person)

▼ **Self-care** (dressing, eating, using the toilet)

▼ **Home living** (housekeeping, preparing food, making and following a schedule)

▼ **Social** (skills for getting along with people)

▼ **Community use** (riding a bus, shopping, attending a movie)

▼ **Self-direction** (making a decision, choosing)

▼ **Health and safety** (basic safety, exercise, good nutrition, illnesses)

▼ **Functional academics** (cognitive abilities that relate to academics applied to daily living)

▼ **Leisure** (developing interests in sports, music, theater, games for public and personal use)

▼ **Work** (learning skills that will lead to a job)

Levels of mental retardation

Some generally accepted terms and IQ ranges will help you understand the levels of mental retardation.

▼ Mild MR is the top of the range with IQs of 55-70.
▼ Moderate means a range of 35 to 55.
▼ Severe includes persons with IQs of 20-35.
▼ Profound is the lowest range of mental retardation.

Mental age

"Mental age" is a good term to know. Mental age is a result of intelligence testing. It means that the child received the same number of correct responses on a standardized intelligence test as an average child at that age in the sample used for the test. But be careful with your terminology. "He has the mind of a four-year-old" is not an appropriate use of the concept of mental age. Say, rather, "His mental age is four years."

Characteristics of the student with mental retardation

Behavioral:

▼ His interests will be more in keeping with his mental age than his chronological age.
▼ He has the same basic emotional needs as the child without MR.
▼ Negative behaviors may be attributed to not knowing, or not understanding the social rules.
▼ His ability to pay attention, or to focus, is limited.
▼ He may be hyperactive (busy) or hypoactive (lethargic).
▼ Routine is important to him.
▼ He quickly forms strong attachments.
▼ He is distractible.

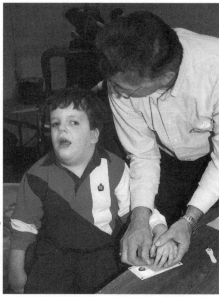

Luke has multiple physical disabilities and mental retardation. Here he enjoys music time with Jan, and craft time with Gaylord. Look carefully; those hands are on the cover!

Educational:

▼ He learns best through experiences that utilize all modalities—touch, sight, hearing, smell, and taste.
▼ He may have physical and/or sensory deficits.
▼ He is a literal thinker; abstract concepts and ideas are difficult for him to grasp.
▼ He doesn't generalize well.
▼ He has poor reasoning skills.
▼ He does not experience a lot of incidental learning.
▼ He often has low self-esteem that affects his motivation and participation.
▼ He is easily confused.

Spiritual:

▼ He loves simply, abundantly, and unconditionally.
▼ He understands spiritual truths.
▼ He is teachable.
▼ He enjoys being with people.
▼ He has a simple faith in God and people.
▼ He and 85 percent of his friends reach a mental age of at least twelve, the age many people become Christians.

Exceptional Teaching Tips

▼ Teach the student with mental retardation in the same classroom with children who do not have mental retardation. The positive examples of good communication and social interaction are good for him.
▼ Create a happy, positive, welcoming classroom.
▼ Stress what the student can do, not what he cannot.
▼ Use vocabulary he will understand, without talking down to him.
▼ Avoid tasks that require skills your student has not acquired, and probably won't acquire, such as advanced reading and writing.
▼ Involve the student in the lesson.
▼ Use repetition—the key to retention.
▼ Overlearning helps overcome memory deficits.
▼ Apply the lesson to the student's everyday life.
▼ Teach in small, logical, sequential steps.
▼ Use motivational techniques such as verbal praise, a sticker, a pat on the back, or a touch on the shoulder.
▼ Use a multisensory approach. Utilize all five senses—sight, smell, touch, taste, and hearing.
▼ Keep tasks simple, but challenge your students.
▼ Give concise, one- or two-stage commands.
▼ Develop a routine.
▼ Encourage independence.
▼ Be consistent, but be flexible.
▼ Be reliable.
▼ Be organized.

A special note

The goal of every teacher is to challenge each student to learn at the peak of his or her capacity. Even the student who learns more slowly than his peers can be assisted to do his best. The right attitude, the right approach, and the right assistance are the keys.

▼ The right attitude: Every student in your class needs to know the material you are presenting. Every child is valuable. Every child can learn.

▼ The right approach: Teach the class as though the student with mental retardation is not there. He is only one member of the class. The adaptations made for him should not weaken the overall effectiveness of the class.

▼ The right assistance: Provide a person to assist the student who has a disability. When his presence seems to interrupt the function of the class, the assistant provides an alternative activity or lesson for him.

Making the negatives positive

For many years, I have used an adaptation of a list in LaDonna Bogardus's *Christian Education for Retarded Persons* (Abingdon Press, 1969) in my classes. You will find the chart on page twenty-eight. The suggestions make it clear how to take the negative edge off the positive learning skills.

Be a friend

Jane Simmons, a special education teacher and a disability ministry specialist, compiled the following information for the Christian Church Foundation for the Handicapped. She makes an important point about being a friend to your students with special needs.

"Most of your students probably have many, many people in their lives—family members, schoolteachers, supervisors, therapists, doctors, case workers—people who either do not have a choice about being involved in their lives, or who get paid to do so. Your students need a friend. They need someone who takes an active interest in their emotional, physical, and spiritual well-being; someone

Jesi has severe mental retardation and does not communicate. Nevertheless, her volunteer buddy Rachel continues to tell her about the love of Jesus.

Making the Negatives Positive

Characteristics that negatively affect learning:	To overcome these negative learning characteristics:
Poor motor control.	Use large muscle activity. Provide activities that develop coordination.
High distractibility.	Avoid exciting activities; limit the number of distracting objects and noises in the classroom.
Limited attention span.	Change tasks frequently; avoid long periods of inactivity.
Poor reasoning ability.	Do not depend on reason. Be explicit with rules and directions.
Difficulty with generalities.	Avoid generalizations; give the specific rather than the general in ideas and vocabulary.
Abstractions have little meaning.	Avoid using symbolism.
Learns slowly.	Use repetition.
Depends on the familiar.	Establish and follow a routine, introduce changes gradually, and strive for consistency in staffing.
Lacks sophisticated communication skills.	Do not hurry expression, help learners use new words, and validate the use of gestures in communication.
Limited powers of retention.	Reiterate ideas and experiences until learning takes place.
Poor self-esteem.	Offer unconditional praise, encouragement, and love.

who provides encouragement and hope because they want to, not because they have to. The unconditional love you share with your students can change their outlook on life and their view of their own personal value and worth in a dramatic way. The mere fact that you have chosen to include a learner with mental retardation speaks volumes to your students and their families about genuine love and acceptance. Your friendship is one of the best gifts you will ever be able to give to your students. As you offer your friendship to the members of your class, be transparent. Share your own hurts, needs, and joys. Let your students know that you value them as friends."

Setting goals for learners with mental retardation

Your goal, in having a student with mental retardation in your class is to help that student learn. The goal isn't to provide a program to please the parents. The goal isn't to baby-sit. The goal is to teach. Your aim is to teach your student:

▼ Who God is
▼ Who His Son, Jesus, is
▼ Who the Old Testament heroes are
▼ The Old Testament events
▼ The New Testament characters
▼ The New Testament events
▼ To appreciate Christian music
▼ To sing Christian choruses and hymns
▼ How to pray
▼ To have relationships with his peers
▼ To know his strengths
▼ To know his self-worth
▼ To be responsible for his own behavior
▼ To accept Jesus as his Lord and Savior

Behavior management

A student with mental retardation will learn better if he behaves well. The goal of classroom discipline is to assist the student in being able to control his own behavior. The following guidelines will help you accomplish this goal:

▼ Have a few clear rules.
▼ Let the class members participate in the formation of the rules.
▼ Post the rules in the classroom and review them often. Remember that some pictures may be needed for clear communication.
▼ Reinforce good behavior.
▼ Don't call attention to the bad.
▼ Do not expect behavior beyond the student's maturity or comprehension.
▼ Model the behavior you expect.
▼ If a student needs some discipline, administer it away from the group.
▼ Before reacting, ask yourself, "What kind of misbehavior is this?"
  – Is it developmental? Teaching methods and behavioral expectations should be geared to the developmental level and learning style of the students.

- Is it attention-getting? If you think the behavior is aimed at getting peer and/or teacher attention, ignore it for the moment. Divert attention. Change the activity. Do something that doesn't focus on the student's behavior. Later, when you can be alone with him, discuss his behavior and offer a consequence if it occurs again.

- Is it defiant and deliberate? Don't lose your cool. Don't use ridicule or sarcasm to correct the behavior. Be firm without being demanding.

- Is it out of control? Is he hysterical, violent, or ready to run away? Approach the student with a quiet, reassuring voice, direct eye contact, arms open. Don't lecture him. Try to distract. Remember: the student who is out of control is often looking for someone to be in control.

Please see more about behavior management on pages sixty-seven through seventy-nine, and the family interview form on page 199.

An Exceptional Life Story

For several months, I observed Pat, a young lady with severe mental retardation, listening to stories about Jesus. She enjoyed them very much, but would never be able to embrace faith. Nonetheless, the Bible truths made a difference in her life. Every Sunday, Pat's young teacher constructed a new visual to illustrate the lesson. Discouraged by the lack of response, she asked me if she should continue her lessons. I urged her to continue and agreed to visit the class the next Sunday.

The lesson for that day, based on Jesus' healing of Peter's mother-in-law, was dramatized with clothespins. Following the lesson, I asked Pat what the lesson was about. Pat laid the clothespin representing Peter's mother-in-law on the table. Slowly, she walked Jesus over to the mother-in-law. She leaned Jesus toward the mother-in-law until the clothespins touched. Popping her lips indicating that Jesus had kissed her, Pat stood the mother-in-law upright. When I asked her who made the mother-in-law well, she responded verbally (a rarity for her), "Jesus." I assured the teacher that her lessons were getting through.

Upon request, Zack was only too happy to display his current project. Note the easily identifiable label on the cupboard behind him. Even nonreaders know how to find needed supplies.

DOWN SYNDROME

Down syndrome is the most recognizable of all the causes of mental retardation. There are three kinds of Down syndrome. The most common (95 percent) chromosomal abnormality is "Trisomy 21." In this case, an extra twenty-first chromosome is present on every cell in the body. Because it happens at conception, the cells develop forty-seven chromosomes instead of the usual forty-six. While the cause is not clear, the mother's age is a risk factor. The second type of Down syndrome, "Translocation," occurs when a piece of the twenty-first chromosome is attached to another chromosome. The third type, "Mosaic," occurs when only some cells in the body have an extra chromosome.

Why is Down syndrome so recognizable?

The physical characteristics are similar from person to person with the disorder. While more than fifty clinical characteristics have been listed, the most common ones are

▼ smaller than their peers without Down syndrome
▼ slanted eyes
▼ folds of skin at the inner corners of their eyes (epicanthal folds)
▼ a flat bridge on the nose
▼ a short neck
▼ a small head
▼ a large, protruding tongue
▼ short, low-set ears
▼ a single crease across the palm of one or both short, broad hands
▼ excessive ability to extend the joints (hyperflexibility)
▼ broad feet with short toes and
▼ more space between the big toe and the next one

Having Down syndrome doesn't stop Danny from marking time for Jennifer as she leads the music time. Someone has clearly taught Danny how to handle those sticks!

There are vision problems:
▼ Drooping eyelids
▼ Cataracts
▼ Tear ducts stop up
▼ Nystagmas (eyes move uncontrollably)
▼ Strabismus (crossed eyes)
▼ Refractive errors

There are hearing problems:
▼ Two thirds have hearing losses.
▼ Both conductive and sensory losses can occur.

There are other health problems:
▼ Two thirds have heart problems.
▼ Hypothyroidism causes obesity.
▼ Teeth come in later, are often missing, or fused and small.
▼ They have dry and scaly skin.
▼ They may have dryness of the eyes.
▼ Inflammation of the lip is common.
▼ They have more diabetes and leukemia.

They develop slowly:
▼ Because they have poor muscle tone, gross motor skills are delayed.
▼ Often they do not sit up until they are twelve months old.
▼ They walk as late as twenty-four months.
▼ While their receptive language is better than expressive, they say their first word at twenty-four months.
▼ The majority of children with Down syndrome will have an IQ around fifty.
▼ They have short-term memory problems.
▼ They are good mimics, perhaps because of their strong visual motor skills.

Are they always happy?
A common stereotype is that children with Down syndrome are happy, loving, and friendly. The truth is they can have the full range of emotional and behavioral problems as children without Down syndrome. In fact, physicians often prescribe medications to control aggressive, oppositional, and other negative behaviors.

Diane Anderson, director of Access Ministries at McLean Bible Church in Virginia, offers the following information to her volunteers when training them how to work with children with Down syndrome.
▼ They experience sensitivity to loud noises or background sounds.
▼ Speech may be hard to understand (because of the over-sized tongue).
▼ Sometimes there is no speech at all.
▼ They can use sign language.
▼ They can be overly stimulated in a nonstructured environment.

▼ They can be stubborn at times.
▼ Making the transition from one activity to the next is difficult.
▼ Challenging behaviors may include throwing, hitting, taking toys from class-mates, or even biting.

Exceptional Teaching Tips

▼ Have a schedule posted in the classroom and be consistent from week to week.
▼ Develop a plan for improving the student's behavior for use when needed.
▼ Create a loving and encouraging classroom; award good behavior.
▼ Use multisensory stations to enhance the lesson for the day.
▼ Encourage creativity during your lesson with dress-up, acting out the story, or singing.
▼ Speak with the child's parents about what he enjoys and try to incorporate his likes into the lesson.
▼ Have a quiet place in the room where a child who feels overwhelmed may go. A corner with a few beanbag chairs and some books and toys would be great.
▼ Most of all, just love them and give lots of hugs.

FRAGILE X SYNDROME

Fragile X syndrome (FXS), sometimes called Martin-Bell syndrome, is the most commonly inherited genetic disorder resulting in mental retardation. It is second only to Down syndrome among the genetic causes of mental retardation. The condition results when the long arm of the X chromosome is broken or weak. Mothers carry the defective gene, and sons are at risk. Daughters are at risk as carriers and for being mildly affected. Boys are more severely affected than girls. Because girls have two X chromosomes, it appears the remaining one compensates for the non-functioning gene. Fragile X syndrome was not widely known in disability circles until the late 1960s when it emerged as a possible cause of autism.

Physical characteristics:

▼ long face
▼ big, prominent ears
▼ double-jointed fingers
▼ flat feet
▼ seizures
▼ heart murmur
▼ hearing problems caused by frequent otitis media (infection or inflammation in the middle ear that can cause a conductive hearing loss; build-up of fluid is a common cause.

▼ eye problems (strabismus, crossed eyes, is the most common)
▼ motor delays

Cognitive characteristics:

▼ mental retardation in boys (ranging from mild to severe)
▼ mental retardation in girls (ranging from mild mental retardation to learning disabilities)
▼ delayed speech
▼ unusual speech pattern (fast, fluctuating rate and repetition of sounds, words, and phrases)
▼ hyperactivity (especially in boys)
▼ attention span problems
▼ learning disabilities
▼ problems with mathematics

Behavioral characteristics:

▼ ranges from socially engaging to autistic-like behavior (boys)
    – avoids eye contact
    – hand-flapping
    – hand-biting
▼ atypical response to sensory stimuli
▼ occasionally aggressive
▼ unusual ways of relating to people
▼ anxious
▼ mood instability

To create a welcoming learning environment, the teacher should be especially sensitive to the fact that the child with FXS needs a structured environment, and will learn better with a good behavior plan in place.

FETAL ALCOHOL SYNDROME

Kim Anderson, a children's ministry worker from Hammond, Indiana, produced the following material on FAS. The mother of two adopted children with FAS, she is also a regional parent representative for InSource; Indiana Resource Center for Families With Special Needs (800-332-4433).

What is fetal alcohol syndrome?

Fetal alcohol syndrome (FAS) is a set of mental and physical disorders that can include mental retardation, brain dysfunction, physical abnormalities, learning disabilities, and psychological disorders. FAS occurs as a result of prenatal exposure to alcohol.

A diagnosis of FAS is based on certain criteria: facial features, small birth weight, central nervous system dysfunction, and a history of prenatal exposure to alcohol. If a baby or child presents all criteria except for the physical features, a diagnosis of Fetal Alcohol Effects (FAE) may be given. In the absence of confirmed maternal drinking, a diagnosis of Alcohol Related Birth Defects (ARBD), or Alcohol Related Neurodevelopmental Disorder (ARND) may be given.

What will the teacher see in a student with FAS?
Physical Characteristics:
▼ Low birth weight
▼ Smaller head circumference
▼ Heart defects
▼ Anomalies to the ears, eyes, liver, or joints
▼ Facial features:
– Epicanthic folds (prolongation of the fold of skin in the upper eyelids)
– Small, widely spaced eyes
– Flat midface
– Short, upturned nose
– Smooth, wide philtrum (space between upper lip and nose)
– Thin upper lip
– Underdeveloped jaw

Facial features will be most prominent between the ages of two and ten.

©2001 Jim West

The child with mental retardation loves simply, abundantly, and unconditionally.

Developmental delays:

▼ Poor motor skills

▼ Learning disabilities

▼ Lower IQ (although not necessarily, as IQ scores from FAS children have been recorded from 15 to 105)

Central nervous system:

▼ Sensory integration problems

▼ Too little or too much muscle tone

▼ Irritability

▼ Poor eating

▼ Poor sleeping

Invisible but serious:

▼ Attention deficits

▼ Memory deficits

▼ Hyperactivity

▼ Difficulty with abstract concepts (for example, math, time, money, faith, the Trinity, Jesus living in your heart)

▼ Poor problem-solving skills

▼ Poor impulse control

▼ Poor judgment

▼ Difficulty learning from consequences

▼ Immature behavior (Social and emotional development in a FAS child is typically three to eight years behind his chronological age. The discrepancy typically widens with age. For example, a five-year-old behaves socially and emotionally like a two-year-old; a ten-year-old behaves like a six-year-old; and an eighteen-year-old behaves like a ten-year-old.)

It is important to note that these characteristics *are not behavior problems*, but are the result of permanent, unchanging damage to the brain. These problems are not always within the student's control. A teacher must recognize and understand the physically based cognitive challenges faced by people with fetal alcohol-related conditions. Without recognition and understanding, the typical, normal behaviors of an FAS child can be misinterpreted as willful misconduct or deliberate disobedience, when it is often just the opposite.

Secondary characteristics such as fatigue, tantrums, irritability, frustration, anger, aggression, fear, anxiety, avoidance, withdrawal, shutdown, and lying can be avoided when parents and teachers understand the cognitive challenges associated with the child's prenatal exposure to alcohol and apply successful interventions to help the child cope.

What do FAS students have difficulty with?

Due to the way an alcohol-affected brain works, children will have difficulty with

▼ Input, or taking in of information
▼ Integration of new information with previous learning
▼ Memory, especially short-term memory
▼ Output, or ability to use information
▼ Cause and effect reasoning—imagination! People with FAS can't imagine something they haven't experienced.
▼ Generalization—they don't have movable parts in the thinking process, so when you change a part of the routine for this student, you create an entirely new routine
▼ Time, telling time, feeling the passage of time, associating specific activities to numbers on a clock
▼ Socialization skills
▼ Independence skills

What methods can a teacher use to control behavior?

When behavior becomes unusual or difficult, it usually indicates an increase in stress, or a feeling of loss of control in a situation, or confusion. Some strategies are helpful:

▼ Try asking, "Do you have something to tell me? Show me? Ask me?"
▼ Have the student change activities.
▼ Decrease the demands placed upon the student.
▼ Allow the student some quiet time in a different area of the room—in a safe place, or with a safe person.

The most important fact to remember is not to take the misbehaviors personally. Remember that the student is not willfully being disobedient, but is trying to function within the confines of what his mind and body will allow.

ADDITIONAL RELATED DIAGNOSES

There are many diagnoses that have mental retardation as a symptom. The following ones are fairly common.

PRADER-WILLI SYNDROME

Prader-Willi syndrome occurs when there is a problem with the fifteenth chromosome. Children have low muscle tone, they overeat, and are obese. Most

have moderate mental retardation; however, some may be lower and a few may be in the normal range. They have small hands and feet. Speech problems are present, especially articulation. They develop slowly, walking and talking later than their typical age-mates.

Suggestion: A teacher needs to be sure to keep food out of the student's sight and monitor compulsive behavior.

ANGELMAN SYNDROME

Angelman syndrome is also a problem with the fifteenth chromosome. Children with AS walk with a stiff gait, have jerky body movements, a wide-smiling mouth, deep-set eyes, and a thin upper lip. They commonly have fair hair and skin and light blue eyes. They have little speech, and experience trouble feeding and sleeping (they don't need as much sleep as their typical age-mates). They have short attention spans. They can be friendly, laugh often, and be very social. They also can be hyperactive. Biting and hair-pulling are often reported. Mental retardation is severe and seizures are common.

Suggestion: A teacher needs an assistant to be responsible for this active, disruptive student.

HYDROCEPHALY

Hydrocephaly is a term common in discussions about mental retardation. The condition is caused by faulty circulation of the cerebral spinal fluid in the cavities of the brain. It can be present at birth, or develop soon afterward. If the pressure isn't relieved, brain damage can be the result. Surgery to install a shunt successfully corrects most of these conditions; however, mental retardation is often present.

Suggestion: The teacher needs to be aware that the student may be restless and easily agitated.

MICROCEPHALY

Microcephaly can be a part of a lot of disorders and syndromes associated with mental retardation. The most common visual feature is a small head. A student with the condition will be more than moderately mentally retarded. The student may have more than usual motor problems, like shuffling when he walks, and have seizures. In most cases the education will be less academic and more about training.

Suggestion: An assistant should be available to the student. He will need extra help with keeping up with the routine and the other students in the classroom.

CRI-DU-CHAT SYNDROME (5P- SYNDROME)

The name means "the cry of the cat." The syndrome is so named because the young child expresses a catlike cry. The syndrome occurs when the short arm of the fifth chromosome is partially deleted. Rather severe mental retardation results. Common characteristics are a small head, loss of muscle tone (hypotonia), wide-set eyes that slant downward with strabismus (the inability of one eye to focus with the other because of an imbalance of muscles), low-set ears, beaked nose, small chin, and short neck. These children reach the developmental milestones late.

Suggestion: Provide the student with an assistant who can take him aside and teach the main point of the lesson.

©Standard Publishing

Erik has microcephaly with all the attending disorders, yet he comes regularly to Sunday school. Here he enjoys a laugh with his teacher Aimee.

NEUROFIBROMATOSIS

Neurofibromatosis occurs once in every four thousand births. It is a genetic disorder that results in recurring benign tumors on the skin, nerves, and sometimes on the internal organs and bones. The noticeable part of the disorder are the tan spots (café-au-lait) that appear on the skin. For most of the people who have it, neurofibromatosis is little more than little bumps on the skin. More serious problems occur when the tumors are on nerves because then, functions are altered. For example, if a tumor occurs on the optic nerve, vision impairment or blindness results. These soft tumors cause deafness, blindness, paralysis, disfigurement, cognitive problems, and seizures. These are the students who need special attention. There is no cure. Cosmetic surgery is used for the tumors.

Suggestion: Help the child understand that true beauty lies within.

CHAPTER 3

Students Who Are
GIFTED

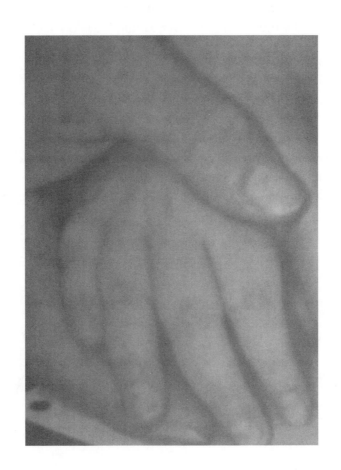

A child who is gifted in a book about kids with special needs? Yes. If "special needs" is defined to include children who function on either side of the mean, then the child who is gifted is as exceptional in his learning abilities as the child with mental retardation is on the other side of the mean.

A common belief is that children who are gifted will achieve their full potential without any assistance. Some of them will do just that. However, most of them will not become all they could become without appropriate assistance.

The child who is gifted should be included and nurtured in the programs of the church school. It is not a difficult task if some basic information is available.

Definition

The definition for gifted children changes from time to time, but is basically derived from the federal definition. The one used by the U.S. Department of Education originated with the Jacob K. Javits Gifted and Talented Students Education Act of 1988. The 1994 reauthorization of the Act (PL 103-382) offers this definition:

"The term 'gifted and talented' when used in respect to students, children or youth, means students, children, or youth who give evidence of high perform-ance capability in areas such as intellectual, creative, artistic, or leadership ability, or in specific academic fields, and who require service or activities not ordinarily provided by the school in order to fully develop such capabilities."

The point of any definition of a child who is gifted is that the child has a more than advanced intellect. In addition to being a leader, he is creative, talented, and artistic.

While the cause of giftedness has been debated for years, it is important to note that children from every walk of life are involved. Children who are gifted and attend our churches need to have special attention given to their spiritual development. They are full of God-given abilities that can be used for good in the kingdom.

The one constant? Each child is unique! Joe is very bright and receives speech therapy. Mary Lou learns from Joe what works, and what doesn't.

©Standard Publishing

The belief that children who are gifted can make it on their own is not the only myth in existence. Other myths are that they have mental instability, are limited in their interests, don't like school, and are nerds. There is also the danger of stereotyping children who are gifted as superhuman. The following list will put those myths to rest. I have added to this list from semester to semester for my course, "Survey of Children With Disabilities." Studying it will give some insights into a child who is gifted.

General characteristics of children who are gifted:
▼ Seem to be superior in every skill: motor, social, emotional, academic, etc.
▼ Are taller, stronger, healthier, more competitive, and more athletic
▼ Read early; many self-taught
▼ Advanced in academics
▼ Are often younger than their classmates
▼ Are happy and well-liked
▼ Have leadership abilities
▼ Have a wide variety of interest
▼ Are well-adjusted, not prone to mental illness
▼ Have high levels of morality
▼ Have a good sense of humor
▼ Learn quickly, are curious, independent, resourceful
▼ Understand the relationship between cause and effect.
▼ Grasp concepts and ideas quickly
▼ Are sensitive to other people and their feelings
▼ Have deep emotional feelings and awareness
▼ Are good in the performing arts

Exceptional Teaching Tips
▼ Recognize the child for who he is, not for his advanced ability.
▼ Don't be intimidated by the child. You have a lot to offer him.
▼ Make him an equal part of the class.
▼ Put his abilities to use in the class, but not at the exclusion of children with lesser gifts.
▼ Provide an on-the-side project to promote spiritual development.
▼ Give the child some outlet to use his gifts in the broader church community. (For example, a nine-year-old who was a master of the violin was often asked to play a solo for church services and be a part of the praise band.)
▼ Encourage attendance at special studies in the church.
▼ Keep the child socially involved with his peers.

An Exceptional Life Story

Kevin could read when he was three. He taught himself. He even learned to type out letters to his parents. By four, his language skills were so advanced that his mother reported, "I think he knows some things I don't." When he entered kindergarten, the skilled teacher kept him with his age-mates, but arranged for more advanced toys and activities for him. In grade school, the special education department provided services that allowed him to develop his outstanding academic abilities.

When he entered high school, he was placed in a mentoring program with a chemist who worked in a local lab. He played quarterback on the high school team. He was president of his class.

The family attended a small church in the community. Because of their deep religious faith, Kevin was also a part of the church activities. His parents reported that from the beginning, "All of his Sunday schoolteachers made him feel a part of the class and he learned about Jesus' love."

During high school, Kevin became a bit bored with his church activities. Two of his old Sunday schoolteachers talked to the minister about the situation. His beginner teacher declared, "We need to see that his abilities are put to use for the kingdom."

The minister had no idea what to do. He called a college friend who was a special educator and explained the situation.

"What are you doing for your private study right now?" asked the educator.

"I am using a study of the book of Luke," responded the preacher.

The educator advised, "Buy Kevin a copy of the book and arrange a time to study with him. Mentor him."

The minister followed the advice. Today Kevin is a minister.

CHAPTER 4

Students With
SPEECH PROBLEMS

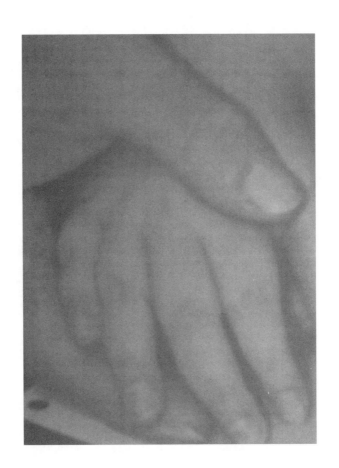

If you have a student with a speech problem in your class, two possibilities exist. First, the student's only disability is a speech problem. Second, the student's speech problem may be a symptom of another disability. Some common diagnoses that often include speech difficulties are cerebral palsy, hearing loss, and cleft lip/palate.

Two factors influence a speech problem: age and hearing. For about 90 percent of the population, speech sounds are learned pretty much on schedule. The following chart will assist you in determining whether or not your student has a speech problem. When you listen to the child's speech, compare it with his age. Typically, we can produce these sounds at the ages shown.

[**p**], [**m**], [**h**], [**n**], and [**w**] appear by age three.
[**b**], [**k**], [**g**], [**d**], [**f**], and [**y**], by four
[**t**], [**ng**], [**r**], [**l**], and [**s**], by six
[**ch**], [**sh**], [**j**], [**th**] (**thumb**), by seven
[**s**], [**z**], [**v**], [**th**] (**feather**), by eight

Good hearing is essential to producing the sounds. Ask the parents if the child's hearing has been checked.

SPEECH DISORDERS

ARTICULATION DISORDERS

Articulation disorders are the largest group of the three speech disorders. In simple terms, the student can't speak plainly. Knowing the four types of articulation disorders will be useful.
▼ In **substitution** the student uses a sound that is easier to produce instead of the correct one. Some examples will clarify:
    – [**w**] for [**r**], "The wabbit is hopping."
    – [**d**] for [**th**], "Doze toys are mine."
    – [**t**] for [**k**], "My pet is a tat."
▼ Often children leave out a sound in a word. A common **omission** is saying "boo" for "blue."
▼ An **addition** is an extra sound in a word. For example, "hammer" becomes "hamber."
▼ **Distortions** occur when the student changes the production of a sound. The listener knows the sound is being made, but it is distorted. "I am going to thleep or zleep," the child announces.

A child whose cleft palate and/or lip has not been surgically corrected will generally have an articulation problem. It will express itself in hyponasality (too little air in the passageway). The child will sound as though he is holding his nose as he talks. In hypernasality, too much air is present in the production of [m], [n], and [ng]. Sometimes there will still be a slight nasality problem after the defect is corrected.

VOICE DISORDERS

Voice disorders are the second of the three speech disorders.

Everyone has a unique voice. The voice is made up of several components:
▼ Pitch (men have lower voice than woman)
▼ Duration (length of time a sound requires)
▼ Intensity (loudness or softness)
▼ Resonance (refers to the way the sound is changed by the mouth, nose, and throat)
▼ Quality (determined by breath support and the condition of the vocal folds)

Voice disorders are often associated with juvenile arthritis, Tourette syndrome, and emotional disorders.

Communication Tips

If the child's speech is too difficult for the listener to understand, the child may use some form of augmented communication. A symbol system, a communication board (home-made or electronic), and synthetic speech devices are a few examples of augmented or alternative communication.

If you have a student who uses a device to assist in communicating, make the process easier by
▼ learning how the device works
▼ allowing the person time to explain
   – enjoying the silence while the person forms questions and comments; trying to fill in for him is a form of interrupting a conversation
   – waiting for the student to finish the statement
▼ looking at the student, not the machine, when you talk
▼ sitting on the student's eye level will make it easier for you and him
▼ not apologizing for saying, "I don't understand"
▼ communicating directly to the student, not through a parent or someone who is with him

DISFLUENCY

Disfluency is the third speech disorder. The most common disfluency problem is stuttering, which is a break in the rhythm of the speech.

▼ When a student stutters, the pattern of the rate and flow of his speech is broken.

▼ While everyone becomes inarticulate at various times—perhaps when under stress or in a hurry—such lack of fluency is not as frequent or severe as in a person with a stutter.

▼ When a person stutters, communication is hampered, talking is uncomfortable for the speaker and his listener, and the speech draws attention to itself.

▼ Children between the ages of three and five are disfluent in the process of normal speech development. Parents are told to ignore it and not name it.

▼ Stuttering often is described by noting that the person repeats sounds. It is more. In addition to the repetitions, there are hesitations, prolongations, blocks, facial grimaces, and extraneous body movement.

▼ The services of a speech pathologist will assist the student in learning to control his stuttering behavior.

While you will not need to alter the way the lesson is presented for most children with speech problems, they do need to know that they are in a positive, welcoming classroom. The following suggestions will aid in creating such an environment:

▼ Respond to the student, not his mispronounced words, the difference in his voice, or his getting stuck on the [t] sound.

▼ Let the student know your classroom is a safe place to talk.

▼ Provide opportunities for the student to practice his speech.

▼ Be a positive speech model for him. Don't tell him how to do it right. Give him a good example.

▼ Look at the student when talking with him.

Something as low-tech as a magnetic alphabet board can be used to help a nonverbal child learn his memory verse.

▼ Give the student time to finish his statements.
▼ Don't fill in the blanks.
▼ Tell other students in the class about the nature of the communication problem their friend has. Teach them that teasing is not acceptable behavior.
▼ Be encouraging and positive to the student.

APRAXIA

Apraxia is a disorder that fits into this section on speech disorders, and could just as well be placed in the learning disabilities section. If a student cannot carry out his plan to move his body from one spot to another without crashing into a chair or a table, or if he cannot move his limbs to write, to zip, or to jump, he is said to have apraxia, or to be apraxic. The mind simply cannot convey the plans to the body. This condition is a result of a poorly functioning proprioceptive system.

Further, if a child recalls the word but cannot voluntarily move the speech apparatus to produce the correct sounds, he has apraxia.

In both the physical sense and the speech/language prospective, there is no paralysis of the muscles.

Words, Words, Words

A discussion about children with speech problems gives us an opportunity to think about two important factors of communication in the disability world: how to talk about disability, and how to talk to a person with a disability. Use the reproducible charts on the following two pages to familiarize yourself with this information, and to share it with others.

Andrea and Katy use a story mat to teach Marcus how much Jesus cares for him. This teaching method is perfect for Marcus, who has apraxia.

How to Talk About Disability

Use the word "**disability**" rather than "**handicap**" to refer to your students with disabilities. "**Handicap**" is the correct word to use when talking about being hampered by architectural barriers or negative attitudes. For example, "Those steps are a handicap to Tyler when he comes to our school."

Avoid the words "**cripple**," "**crippled**," "**deaf and dumb**," "**slow**," "**crazy**," "**invalid**," "**acts funny**," and other insensitive, archaic descriptions of disability. In the same vein, expressions like "**afflicted with**," "**a victim of**," and "**suffer from**" lead to pity and sympathy, not respect and acceptance.

Use people-first language. Don't say, "**the disabled**," "**the retarded**," "**the cerebral palsied**," "**a paraplegic**." Rather say, "Jim has cerebral palsy." "Joey has autism." "They are people with disabilities." "Ann has a vision problem."

Don't speak of your student in special, overly courageous, exceptionally brave, or super-human terms.

Refer to devices that assist mobility and otherwise enable people in a kind and gentle manner. Choose "**Jacob uses a wheelchair**" rather than "**Jacob is confined to a wheelchair**"; "**Emily uses sign language**" instead of "**Emily talks with her hands**"; "**Michael communicates with an electronic machine**" (or the specific name of the device) instead of "**Michael uses a machine to talk**."

When conveying that a student in the class does not have a disability, stay away from the word "**normal**." The terms "**typical**" or "**a child without a disability**" are kinder and more accurate. Don't overdo such concepts as "**Well, we all have a disability of some kind**." The person dealing with the loss of one of his five senses, or a physical problem that impedes his mobility and/or requires assistive devices will not find that comforting.

How to Talk to a Person With a Disability

The second facet of our communication skills with students with disabilities is our ability to talk with them. Again, what you do as a teacher will be reflected in your students without disabilities. You are their role model. Some basic suggestions will be useful.

▼ Don't assume that a student with a disability other than a hearing loss can't hear. Often we respond to a person with a disability by talking louder.

▼ Don't assume that people with speech, hearing, or physical problems have cognitive problems as well. In other words, don't treat them as if they were less intelligent than you are.

▼ Don't apologize for not understanding a student's speech. Just ask the person to repeat what he said.

▼ Don't say you understand someone's speech when you don't. Develop a friendly response: "My ears aren't working right today—will you say that again?" "Run that by me again, please."

▼ If the speech is difficult to comprehend, learn to listen for the subject of the conversation. Words like "Mom," "Dad," "church," "school" will focus your understanding; then listen for action words like "went," "walked," "saw."

▼ If push comes to shove, use pencil and paper, or gesture wildly. Work to get the message. Your students will learn a valuable lesson from their teacher.

▼ Talk directly to the person, not through a companion or family member.

▼ As you work with the student, the communication problems will diminish. The comprehension level will increase and a chat becomes fun. You may find that the members of the class learn to understand their friend faster than you do. I have often used children as translators.

CHAPTER 5

Students With
LANGUAGE PROBLEMS

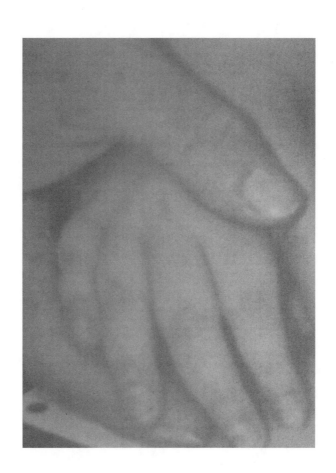

Speech means producing the sound. Language means understanding the code that a group of people (in our case, English-speaking people) have decided to use to govern the way they talk.

You could have a student in your class who speaks fine, but has trouble with the code. The following information will help you assess the problem and offer some help.

A student who has good language skills has some things going for him.
▼ He hears well.
▼ He has good cognitive skills. We recognize these good skills through the following factors:
 – He hears and understands what is said to him.
 – He has good memory.
 – He understands concepts, like prepositions (in, off, out, up).
 – He can recall words and ideas.
▼ He lives in a stimulating environment, which means that he has good language models and he has his communication needs met.

Speech is the way we produce sound. Language is the code we use to interrupt the speech. A student may have a speech problem without having a language problem. He may have a language problem without having a speech problem.

For example, I say, "pig." When I articulate these two consonants and this vowel, the result is "pig." When my listener hears "pig," she thinks of an animal with a curly tail that says "oink, oink." There's more. From the pig we get bacon, ham, and sausage. The student with a language problem will not associate the sound of the word "pig" with the animal that oinks, or the bacon, ham, and sausage.

©Standard Publishing

Christina has no verbal communication,

but her warm smile and sparkling eyes easily

convey that she is glad to be in church.

55

Language development like speech production is progressive and sequential. The chart on the next page will give you an idea of where young children are in their use of language for the first five years of their lives. It will also give you a listening guide. You can then evaluate where your student is in his language development. Some may be at a higher level than indicated on the chart, others will be at a lower level. The chart will give you a gauge.

TYPES OF LANGUAGE PROBLEMS

RECEPTIVE LANGUAGE DISORDERS

Processing language has to do with hearing what is said and making sense from it. When a student has a problem in receiving and processing the words he hears, he has difficulty understanding what is being said to him. It will appear that these children aren't paying attention. Some teachers would say, "He didn't hear a word I said." The fact is, he did, but he couldn't process what you meant.

EXPRESSIVE LANGUAGE DISORDERS

When a child has difficulty using spoken language, or composing a response, his language problem is expressive. These children often don't know a lot of words and tend to use the same words and expressions over and over. Their speech is immature. Gesturing is often a part of their attempts to express themselves.

COMBINATION EXPRESSIVE/RECEPTIVE

When receptive language age is below age level and the expressive language is lower still, the child has a mixed language disorder.

Language Development

By six months
The child will use a different cry when he is hungry, needs to be changed, or is bored!
Laughs.
Coos in response to familiar happenings.
Knows the difference in voices and other environmental sounds.

By twelve months
Knows his/her name.
Understands "No."
Babbles.
Recognizes the names of people and objects in his world.
Responds to simple commands, "Come here," "Give me the ball."
Will mimic motor acts, like waving bye-bye.

By eighteen months
Says the names of objects.
Points to pictures in a book.
Jabbers, but says single, understandable words.
Uses speech as a social tool.
Can have up to a fifty-word vocabulary.
Knows more words and directions.
Knows three or four body parts; "Where is your nose?"

By twenty-four months
Puts two or three words together.
Is starting to use the parts of speech
Uses some verbs (go, ride)
    Simple adjectives and adverbs (small, good)
    May understand but not obey simple commands.
Vocabulary has expanded to three hundred words.
Pays more attention to others talking to him.
Uses plurals.

By thirty-six months
Vocabulary is up to one thousand words.
Tells about activities.
Asks some questions.
Understands prepositions (on, over, up, beside).
Takes turns while talking with a buddy.
Knows objects by what he does with them. "I sleep in my bed."
Completes two-stage directions.

By forty-eight months
Vocabulary is up to fifteen hundred words.
Can tell stories, made up and real.
Uses the question words, "who, where, what, when, and how."
Understands more complex sentence structures and
    uses a few of his own.
Enjoys listening to stories.
Often asks, "Why?"

By sixty months
You are dealing with a master of language!
Uses connective words (the, and, but).
Sentences are more complex.
Is getting good at using the past tense.
On request can give his full name, sex, street address, and telephone number.

APHASIA

When a child has difficulty using language and there has been injury to his brain, aphasia is often the diagnosis. Many students with traumatic brain injury have aphasic problems. Aphasia may be referred to as expressive or receptive.

Additional information regarding language problems:

▼ The child should be able to produce sounds that are understood by his listener (phonology more than articulation).
▼ The child should be able to put a sentence together with the correct grammar (morphology and syntax).
▼ The child should speak in sentences that are meaningful and relate to what is going on (semantics).
▼ The child should know the rules for using language in a variety of contexts (pragmatics).

DEVELOPMENTAL LANGUAGE DELAY

Some children will have a delay in language usage that is not a disorder. The child simply does not acquire the skills in a neat, sequential schedule. An enriched environment helps the situation, and by the time these children go to school they are fine—using speech and language on schedule.

Some of this group have more serious problems and will require therapy and often need some help with reading during the school years.

BILINGUAL COMMUNICATION PROBLEMS

Because more and more children living in the United States are bilingual, it is important for their teachers to know that speech and language problems can develop. I have a granddaughter who lives in Germany with parents who speak English. She had to have therapy to correct a language problem. It is easy to understand that the development of the sounds and codes of two languages would be a bit of an overload on the brain.

Exceptional Teaching Tips
Create a relaxed atmosphere.
▼ Don't be uptight when the words don't flow smoothly.
▼ Don't ask the child to do anything that is above his language ability.
▼ Encourage his fellow classmates to be helpful and patient.
▼ Convey your understanding and willingness to help.
▼ Be a role model for good language usage.

Give the child a reason to use language.
▼ Decorate the room with attractive pictures and objects that will trigger reactions in the child.
▼ Use role play that will give the child opportunities to respond.
▼ Use games that encourage the use of language.

Be a good language teacher.
▼ Praise the child's attempts to use language.
▼ Instead of correcting his language by saying "You should have said," just say, "Yes, Joe," and offer the correct usage.
▼ Don't ask a lot of questions. They put the student on the spot.
▼ If the class is responding to a question, create a simple yes or no question for the child with a language problem such as, "Chad, do you think that is a good answer?" Give him a boost—it will pay off.
▼ Create language moments. I know a great teacher who thinks aloud for her students with language impairments. I recall a lesson when she said, "I wonder how dogs feel when their masters pat their heads." She began to respond to her own question with a long list of answers: happy, warm inside, wags his tail, and on she went. A little guy who rarely spoke interrupted with, "He licked my hand."
▼ Encourage the use of complete sentences. When asking for information, ask the children in your class to express themselves in full sentences. For example, "My name is Shannon," encourages more language, than "Shannon."
▼ Tap the rhythm of the memory work.

©Standard Publishing

Mac is just beginning to communicate verbally. For now, he uses a Magna Doodle to express his thoughts and needs. When you look at the photos of Mac on pages 76 and 77, you will see that he keeps it with him at all times.

CHAPTER 6

Students With
EMOTIONAL AND
BEHAVIOR PROBLEMS

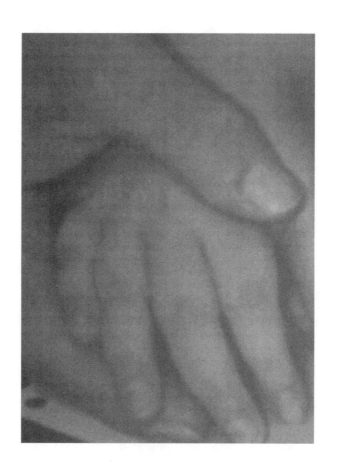

People with emotional and behavioral problems are first and foremost people. They need the love and respect of others in their lives. They can be an intimidating group primarily because of misunderstanding. True, they can be a handful, but having some information and developing some insights regarding their behavior will go a long way in including them in your class.

Some facts about children with these problems:
▼ There are more boys than girls.
▼ Boys tend to be more externalizing, girls, internalizing. (This is covered in greater detail on pages sixty-seven and seventy-eight.)
▼ The most common behavioral problem is acting-out.
▼ They do not always grow out of it.
▼ They don't do well in school.
▼ They have trouble passing competence exams.
▼ They often drop out of school.
▼ They are worthy of love and attention.

IDEA definition
Emotional disturbance is one of the disability categories in IDEA under which children may receive special education services.

Study the following definition from IDEA. Knowing this information will help you relate better to the student in your class. You will know that the emotional problem isn't temporary. It is bothering one of the most vital parts of his life, his education.

I.   The term means a condition exhibiting one or more of the following characteristics over a long time, and to a marked degree that adversely affects educational performance:
(a) A student's inability to learn that cannot be explained by intellectual, sensory, or other health factors,
(b) An inability to build or maintain satisfactory interpersonal relation ships with peers and teachers,
(c) Inappropriate types of behavior or feelings under normal circum stances,
(d) A general pervasive mood of unhappiness or depression,
(e) A tendency to develop physical symptoms or fears associated with personal or school problems.
II. The term includes schizophrenia. The term does not apply to those who are socially maladjusted, unless it is determined that they have an emotional disturbance.

It is important to stress that the emotional problem is noticeable (to a marked degree) and will not go away over a long period of time.

CLASSIFICATION OF EMOTIONAL AND BEHAVIOR DISORDERS

Classifying emotional and behavior disorders is not easy. Following is a list of the ones that will most likely be a part of an educational setting.

ANXIETY DISORDER

Anxiety disorder is the most common childhood disorder in this category. The basic characteristic is that the child has excessive fears and worries. There are six common expressions of anxiety disorder.

▼ **Obsessive-compulsive disorder** Child is obsessed with repetitive thoughts of being sick, dying, or some other malady; he is compulsive in repetitive behaviors such as counting, repeating phrases, and washing hands.

▼ **Phobias** Child has unfounded fear toward an object, situation, event.

▼ **Panic disorder** Child's panic attacks result in physical symptoms like sweating, dizziness, racing heart.

▼ **Generalized anxiety disorder** Child has excessive fears unrelated to any prior event.

▼ **Posttraumatic stress disorder** Child recalls a distressing occurrence such as violence, abuse, severe weather, etc.

▼ **Eating disorders** include **anorexia nervosa**, which means the person does not take in enough food to maintain an appropriate body weight, and **bulimia nervosa**, which means the person binge eats and then vomits. Both disorders are the result of fear of gaining weight.

ANXIETY-WITHDRAWAL DISORDER

These students are shy, self-conscious, unsure of themselves, anxious, depressed, reticent, want to retreat into the background, and have low self-esteem. They are not aggressive.

BIPOLAR DISORDER

▼ Is also referred to as manic-depressive.
▼ Is found in children as well as adults.
▼ Is characterized by mood swings.
▼ Often runs in families.
▼ During the depressed stage, the child will display some of the following behaviors:
  – He feels sad and anxious, worthless, guilty, hopeless.
  – He lacks energy.
  – He has poor concentration and memory.
  – He loses interest in regular activities.
  – His sleep is disturbed.
  – His appetite can be ravenous or lost.
▼ During the manic stage, the child will respond in a variety of ways:
  – He is on top of the world.
  – His behaviors are unusual for a while.
  – He is irritable.
  – He is distracted.
  – He has lots of energy.
  – He talks rapidly.
  – He is agitated.
  – He sleeps less.
  – He makes poor judgments.

MAJOR DEPRESSION

Depression can happen at any age. It happens to kids. The main symptoms are feeling sad and useless, crying a lot, losing interest in friends, activities, and school, not eating or sleeping well, not taking care of basic hygiene, thinking he can't do anything right, and feeling an overwhelming sense of hopelessness. Depression is often hard to detect in children. The key is any change that is noted in their attitudes and activities.

OPPOSITIONAL-DEFIANT DISORDER

▼ A student with this disorder is rude, negative, disobedient, and aggressive.

▼ The disorder expresses itself in blaming someone else for failures, arguing with adults, defying authority figures, using bad language, being vindictive, acting irritable, and displaying signs of low self-esteem.

▼ The cause is real. The student is not being deliberate in his behaviors. The cause could be inherited. It is likely neurological, maybe a chemical imbalance.

▼ An important part of therapy is positive attention from caring adults.

CONDUCT DISORDER

Students with conduct disorders are not difficult to recognize. They demonstrate aggressive and disruptive behavior. They hit, throw, tease, fight, and act defiant. They are uncooperative, rude, quarrelsome, inattentive, and irresponsible.

The milder the disorder the more likely it can be handled in a regular educational setting. The more difficult ones are likely to be removed and educated/treated in a restrictive placement. Sadly, more severe cases continue into adulthood.

SCHIZOPHRENIA

Because schizophrenia is a widely recognized emotional disorder, you may have questions about it. In short, the disorder causes people to lose contact with reality, sense things that do not exist, have feelings of grandeur, or feelings that everyone is against them, and can't enjoy the pleasures of life. While the disorder can be seen in the adolescent years, it is extremely rare in children.

Zack has bipolar disorder and emotional issues, but here he is clearly engrossed in working with Rosemary to make a bed that will lower the paralyzed man to see Jesus.

©Standard Publishing

TIC DISORDERS

There are several tic disorders. The most widely known one is **Tourette syndrome** (TS)

▼ TS is an inherited, neurological disorder characterized by repeated involuntary movements and uncontrollable vocal sounds called tics. Boys are affected more than girls. An estimated one hundred thousand Americans have TS. Symptoms range from mild to severe. The disorder doesn't affect intelligence. The tics decrease with age. Some people improve to the point they discontinue the use of medication.

▼ Motor tics may include eye blinking, facial grimacing, shoulder shrugging, fast extension of the arms, sticking the tongue out, stretching movement, and the like.

▼ Vocal tics may include clearing the throat, grunting, snorting, sniffing, coughing, humming, barking, and spitting, and in a few cases, offensive words and phrases.

▼ There are other problems including the full range of emotional disorders, especially obsessive-compulsive disorder, learning disabilities, problems with reading and math, attention deficit disorder, and stuttering.

Diane Anderson's volunteers in Access Ministries at McLean Bible Church in Virginia, are taught the following facts to help children with TS.

▼ Provide a consistent schedule in the classroom.

▼ Be consistent with discipline.

▼ Create a socially active classroom by providing positive opportunity for interaction with each other.

▼ Notice when the student is doing well and praise him.

▼ Use at least two other class members to serve as buddy to the student with TS.

▼ Provide interactive opportunities for the class to participate in the lesson, such as music, acting out the story, or art.

Understanding externalizing and internalizing

In order to understand how to deal with students with emotional and behavior problems, you must be aware of two widely accepted categories of behavior disorders: externalizing and internalizing.

Externalizing takes place when a person is unable to take responsibility for his own actions, or fails to see the connection between behavior and consequences. Externalizing will be characterized by

▼ a lot of arguing and noncompliant behavior when asked to do something

▼ aggressiveness toward people and things

▼ temper tantrums

▼ lying and/or stealing

▼ inability to control himself or his behaviors

▼ making other students submit to him by force, both physical and verbal

▼ so aggressive that he doesn't develop good relationships with his peers

Internalizing happens with a person who seems unhappy and feels uptight about life. He is down on himself and displays a general aura of negativism. Internalizing will be characterized by

▼ feelings of worthlessness, sadness, and depression
▼ dwelling on the same thought or event
▼ frequent crying
▼ hearing and seeing things that aren't there
▼ feelings of anxiety that result in complaints of headaches or other somatic problems
▼ talk of taking his life
▼ loss of interest in activities
▼ signs of withdrawal that keep him from having good relationships
▼ the child's peers tease, ignore, or actually abuse him

Whatever the name of the emotional or behavior problem, if the teacher knows if she is dealing with a student who acts out or a student who keeps his feelings inside, the process of making the classroom a good place for him will be easier.

Causes

"He is just mean!" "He does that on purpose!" Teachers will feel better if they understand that the student is not deliberately acting the way he does. There is a reason. Looking over a list of some reasons for emotional problems will help in the process of dealing with the student.

▼ Genetics
▼ A difficult birth
▼ Childhood illness (She was OK until she had _____.)
▼ Traumatic brain injury
▼ Injury to the central nervous system
▼ Abnormalities in the brain
▼ Inherited predispositions
▼ Early traumatic experience
▼ Chemical imbalance
▼ Learned bad behavior
▼ Doesn't learn adaptive behaviors
▼ Environmental problems

Some special words of advice

Don't blame parents for their child's behavior. Working together to benefit the student is more useful than stereotyping the parents. In most cases, the parents are concerned and are at their wit's end in knowing what to do to help the child they love so deeply.

It is easy to be critical of medications because of overuse, lack of adequate supervision, or reports of addiction. However, there are great medicines that can and do make a positive difference in a child's life. If you suspect that a certain medication is causing some problems, report your suspicions. When the physician monitors the medication using feedback from the family and/or caregiver, the results will be better for the child.

CHILD ABUSE

It is a heartbreaking fact that in our society today you probably will work with children whose emotional problems are caused by abuse. According to data from the National Clearinghouse on Child Abuse and Neglect, there were an estimated 826,000 victims of abuse in 1999. That is a rate of 11.8 victims per one thousand children. These figures support the estimate that one boy in five and one girl in three is the victim of abuse. Children with disabilities are even more prone to be abused.

Abuse occurs when the parent or caregiver responsible for the child's welfare abuses, neglects, or fails to prevent acts that result in serious harm, death, emotional abuse, physical abuse, sexual abuse, or exploitation.

©Standard Publishing

Roughhousing with his buddy Isaac lets off some steam for Christian, who has oppositional-defiant disorder. Then he can sit quietly and help Andrea pick out songs for music time.

A child who has been abused may indicate it by lack of trust in the adults in his life, by poor grades in school, by not seeking new friendships, by withdrawal, by a poor self-image, and by aggressive behavior, from mild to severe.

The child whose abuse prevented his bonding with loving adults as an infant may have an attachment disorder, which makes it hard for him to be sensitive to people around him. Our brains need to be nurtured by loving, caring people. This stimulation aids normal development.

Exceptional Teaching Tips

The teacher of children who have been abused must be aware of the power of example, and the impact she has on the child.

▼ The teacher must be a model of togetherness and self-control.
▼ The teacher should give and receive affection.
▼ The teacher is firm but fair.
▼ The teacher radiates hope, joy, and assurance.
▼ The teacher believes in the child.
▼ The teacher believes that what she is doing will make a difference.
▼ The teacher is a good listener.
▼ The teacher is willing to alter methods and approaches.

Effective discipline

▼ Be full of praise.
▼ Use another adult or a class member to attend to the person's behavior outburst.
▼ Make sure what you expect is clear.
▼ Be kind in correcting.
▼ Do not humiliate.
▼ Do not lose your temper.
▼ Admit it if you are wrong.
▼ Be consistent.
▼ Be fair.
▼ Apologize if you blew it. (Hearing your apology will help the child develop a skill he needs to acquire.)
▼ Do not be intimidated by the student or his family.
▼ Ignore a behavior if it is bothering you more than the class.
▼ Don't pity or show sympathy for the student. It suggests superiority.
▼ Recognize and admit when it is time to have a respite from the student.
▼ Discover the child's hobbies or special interests and surprise him by referring to them in class.
▼ Develop a positive relationship.

The Classroom

▼ Seat the student with the behavior disorder so that you can see him.

▼ Keep him an "arm's length" away from the closest student.

▼ Keep the classroom as clutter-free as possible.

▼ Keep objects and materials out of sight or reach. It helps keep temptation away.

▼ Establish classroom rules and consequences, and post them.

▼ Create an emotionally safe classroom.

▼ Use a lot of drama, music, art, and other ways a student can express himself.

▼ Have a place for the student to calm down (a beanbag corner, a tent).

Biting

Teachers often ask, "What do I do with a child who bites?" The answer is not to bite him back. Dealing with biting requires understanding, patience, and time. Biting will naturally occur with babies and toddlers and its incidence will increase when children are in groups. Biting is normal, though not pleasant, and will stop with time.

The Access Ministry at McLean Bible Church offers some solid advice found on page seventy-two.

Biting

Biting may occur for the following reasons:
▼ The child's language is limited, so rather than using words, he uses teeth.
▼ The child is teething and is very conscious of his mouth. To him, a warm body is a good place to try to put new teeth.
▼ Biting elicits immediate and obvious reactions from adults and other children.
▼ Biting is very difficult to prevent because it happens quickly and often for no discernable reason. It is one of the few times the child, not the adult, has power.

General information
▼ Children who bite are not by nature "mean" and should not be labeled as "bad," "mean," or "a biter." Children generally live up to the expectation of the adults or children around them.
▼ Biting seems to go in spurts. Weeks can go by without an incident, but the behavior may surface suddenly.
▼ Biting is most prevalent between the ages of fifteen to thirty months, although it can occur at a younger age or with older preschoolers.
▼ Unless the skin is broken, the wound does not need medical attention. The skin will bruise and will heal with time.

What to do when a child bites
▼ Tell the biter very firmly and with appropriate language, "NO BITING! Biting hurts."
▼ Comfort the injured child.
▼ Inform the parent of the biting child about the incident. Both sets of parents will appreciate kindness, compassion, and reassurance.

Advice for parents
▼ Understand that biting is normal at certain ages, although unpleasant.
▼ Believe that the volunteers are doing all that they can to help the children (biters and bitees) through the situation.
▼ Do not ask who is doing the biting. If you know who it is, do not mention his or her name in front of your child or others.
▼ Never blame or confront the parents of a biting child. They would do anything to stop the behavior, and frequently are more distressed than the parents of a bitten child.
▼ When playing with a child, avoid "nibbling" or pretending to bite.

CHAPTER 7

Students With
AUTISM

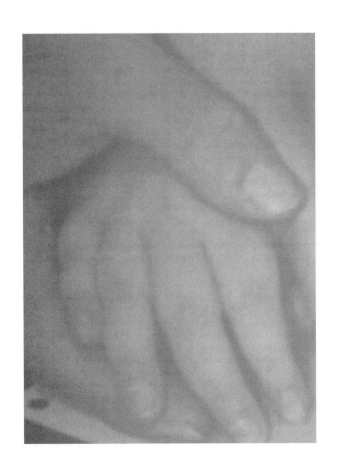

At almost every workshop I have done during the past few years, Sunday school-teachers have asked for help in dealing with students with autism. Autism has become more widely known than it was a few years ago, publicized by formal studies, by teacher reports, and by media specials. IDEA has given it its own special education category. It has gone from a rare disorder to a common one. More boys have autism than girls. Children with autism are diagnosed by the time they are thirty months old.

In addition to the label of autism, a student may carry the following labels:
▼ **Pervasive developmental disorder**—not otherwise specified (PDD-NOS) is used if a child has some symptoms of autism, but not enough to carry the classical diagnosis.
▼ **Asperger's syndrome** describes children with autistic behaviors, but who have good language skills.
▼ **Childhood disintegrative disorder** (CDD) is used with children who appear to be developing normally for a few years, but then lose skills, and show autistic-like behaviors.
▼ **Rett syndrome** means the child has inadequate brain growth, has seizures and autistic behaviors. It happens to girls.

Autism may occur with fragile X syndrome, Tourette syndrome, learning disabilities, and ADHD.

An Exceptional Life Story
One of my favorite children with autism is Casey. I have known him all of his life. He is a good example of a child with autism. He loves books. If the book has been read to him, he likely has it memorized. Once he handed me a book and said, "Page nineteen." When I looked at the page, he said every word just as it was written. He can tell the make and model of any car he sees. I enjoy him. It is obvious that he is aware that I am in his world, but he leaves no hint of that. He doesn't give me eye contact. Once we were walking down a hallway together. It wasn't planned—we just happened to be going the same way at the same time. I said, "Hi, Casey." He didn't seem to hear me and he certainly left no sign of noticing me until he said, "Mr. Jim, that's a fire extinguisher. It is used to put out fires." He receives speech therapy, special education services, and regular education services. He is a faithful member of his Sunday school class and other children's programs at his church.

His parents, Penny and Jody Rood, describe their son this way: "In our thoughts, Casey presents a myriad of images. Strikingly handsome, with a beautiful smile, a blessing of healthfulness, sometimes offering himself to be hugged and sometimes the giver of strong hugs. He is a real teaser with an emerging sense of humor, a lover of his books and magazines. (The publishers of *Readers Digest* would be shocked at the distance some of their monthly issues have gone at our house.) He also loves cars, videos, and computer programs. He begs his brothers to play Nintendo so he can watch and listen, but he never wants to handle the controller himself. He is an amazing imitator of sounds, whether living or mechanical. Our hindsight tells us we should have purchased stock in certain food items but certainly not vegetables. He keeps us all on his schedule and expects a full briefing of any diversions from that schedule. At times he stretches our patience, but he has been and continues to be an instrument in the development of our love, compassion, humility, gentleness, and kindness. We are indeed thankful to be blessed with Casey."

The most widely accepted definition of autism is the one used by the IDEA: "A developmental disability significantly affecting verbal and nonverbal communication and social interaction, usually evident before age three, that adversely affects a child's educational performance."

Some other characteristics often associated with autism are
▼ engagement in repetitive activities and stereotyped movements,
▼ resistance to environmental change or change to daily routines, and
▼ unusual responses to sensory experiences.

That's the textbook definition; here is what you are likely to see in the classroom:
▼ **Communication deficits.** The student may not speak, may have limited use of language, may use repetitive phrases, or carry on a nontypical conversation. Abstract concepts will give him trouble.
▼ **Relational deficits.** The student will not relate appropriately to people, events, and objects. Often he will avoid eye contact. Events and objects, unless they are something he likes, will be equally detached from his attention.
▼ **Ritualistic activities.** He will play for long periods of time with one object. A book, a spoon, a piece of string will occupy the child's attention for hours.

▼ **Rigid adherence to routine.** Any change in schedule—how silverware is placed on the table, which sweater he wears—will get a reaction, often a loud one.

▼ **Atypical reactions to the sensory.** Loud noises, bright lights, textures of food, the fabric of his clothes, all will receive marked attention.

▼ **Repetitive movements and behaviors.** He will flap his hands, flip his fingers in front of his eyes, or do some similar movement. The activity probably relates to the overload from sensory information that he can't handle.

▼ **Lack of creativity.** The student with autism will not be creative, imaginative, or initiate games.

The chart on page seventy-eight illustrates the behaviors a child with autism will display in an educational sitting. It was adapted by a student of mine, Alicia Lauvray, who is now a case manager in a facility in Ohio.

Exceptional Teaching Tips

▼ Don't let the student's behavior overwhelm you. Working with his parents, arrange a plan for dealing with his behavior. Target the behaviors that are the most disrupting to the class.

▼ Involve the student in the class. Find a task he can do.

▼ Develop a picture and word schedule for the routine of the class. It will be especially useful when the student changes from one routine to another.

▼ Use his peers to interest him and demonstrate appropriate behavior.

▼ Train an assistant to work with the child.

▼ Don't pressure the student to do things that he doesn't want to do. Give him a choice.

▼ Develop a special handshake, a word, or a gesture and use it every time you greet your student.

©Standard Publishing

*A guy with autism just needs a buddy. In this class, Dale helps Mac keep his mind on the tasks at hand. This teacher has planned an exceptional multi-sensory lesson. The children first **read** the names of the books of the Bible, then **copy** one name onto a sheet of paper, then **stand** in a circle to place the books in order, then go around and **say** or **sing** the names of the books of the Bible.*

SIGNS AND SYMPTOMS OF AUTISM

Has difficulty mixing with other children

Indicates needs by gesture

Acts deaf

Is not cuddly

Resists learning

Avoids eye contact

Has no fear of real dangers

Manifests inappropriate attachment to objects

Giggles and laughs inappropriately

Spins objects

Is markedly overactive or underactive

Plays intently for abnormally long periods

Resists change in routine

Has a standoffish manner

▼ Avoid asking, "Would you like to color these pictures?" Say rather, "We are going to color these pictures. We are so excited!" Approaching the student with a plan in mind keeps him from having to decide. Remember, he thinks in pictures and it takes him a little while to get them all in place. He probably wants to color, but has not arrived at that point. You make the decisions and he will (probably) follow the plan!

▼ Keep your classroom as structured as possible.

▼ Try to maintain the same routine. If there is a change, tell the student with autism in advance. If he is prepared, the change will be easier.

▼ Follow the parents' and school's leads in dealing with ritualistic behaviors. Everyone in the student's life should use the same approach.

▼ Give the student time to adjust to his new classroom space and the people in it.

▼ Prepare him for the experience. Take him to the classroom when no one else is there. Talk to him about what will happen. Show him the picture schedule on the wall.

▼ As time goes by, expect more of the student.

▼ Because he may not enjoy being touched or having you invade his space, don't approach him directly. Without looking at him, sort of back into his space. It works for me.

▼ When orienting the other members of the class about their classmate with autism, tell them he doesn't always look at them and he might pull away when they touch him. This is just a part of having autism. As he gets to know them, he might look at them more and not be bothered by being touched. Stress with the children that their friend with autism knows they are there and is happy about it.

The Notebook System

Because the Christian education program is a different environment for the child with autism, check with his parents or school to see if there is something you can do to help him meet a goal he is trying to achieve. For example, Casey, who attends our Sunday school and children's church, has the goal of becoming less dependent on prompts. To help him accomplish this goal, his public school-teacher developed an icon for each activity on his schedule and placed them in a loose-leaf notebook on Velcro strips. "Computer Time," "Math Lesson," and "Library" are some examples. When the student is ready to do the next activity, he opens the notebook, removes the icon and places it in the middle of a star on the front of the notebook. He collects the materials he needs and starts the activity. Instead of telling him what to do, the teacher simply touches the icon to remind him of the schedule.

At church the same approach was developed. The notebook developed for Casey contains two pages—one for Sunday school and one for children's church. The Sunday school page has six icons: Prayer, Review, Bible Story, Activity, Offering, and Project. If the Sunday schoolteacher decides to alter the schedule, she or the student's assistant arranges the icons accordingly.

How to Teach the Student With Autism

Prepare to teach the child with autism by making three visits:
▼ one to his home
▼ one to his school
▼ and with him

Notice his behavior at home.
▼ How does he interact with family members, his toys, and his environment?
▼ How does he communicate with the family members?
▼ How does he occupy his time? Ask his parents if he has an unusual attachment to something. It can be a crayon, aluminum foil, or a toy.
▼ Find out what sensory experiences cause him to react: a light being turned on, the sound the furnace makes when it comes on, sirens from the street. Inquire about his eating habits. Children with autism often prefer one food and are bothered by the texture of some food items.

Observe his behavior at school.
Because of confidentiality, the parents will have to approve your visit to the school. Generally, teachers will be glad to have you. They know that the more consistent the child's instruction and behavior management can be in his various environments, the better he will do.
▼ Observe the techniques the teachers use at school.
▼ Adopt their behavior control methods.
▼ Take note of what the teacher is doing to help the student organize his world.

After you have made these visits, arrange a time that you can visit with the child.
▼ Find out a place he likes to go.
▼ Take a couple of members of your Sunday school class. A trip to the zoo, a walk in the park, an hour at the playground, or a stop at the ice cream parlor will provide you firsthand information about the new student in your class.

The children's church page has seven icons: Opening Prayer, Offering, Game, Songs, Prayer Time, Bible Story, and Activity. This notebook system helps the child with autism to feel in control of his environment, and helps him to focus on what he is supposed to be doing. If his mind wanders, he can remind himself with a glance where he is and what is going on.

Britiney, the student teacher who developed a notebook for Casey's use at church, reported the following results the first Sunday he used it: "Driving to church with the newly finished notebook, I was excited, and also a little scared. What if he didn't make the connection between this notebook and the one at school? What if there were activities that I didn't have an icon for, and he couldn't deal with the change in routine? I prayed, 'God, please help this to go the way it's supposed to.' Everyone who worked with Casey—his parents, teachers, and helpers—was excited to see this new system get under way. We all hoped Casey would be just as excited. I went to his Sunday school class to explain the notebook to this teacher and to the assistant. Casey hadn't arrived.

"When I returned after Sunday school, Casey and the other children were waiting at the door to come in for church. Casey was in front of the line, notebook in hand. The report was that the notebook had worked. Casey had known immediately what to do. He had put the music icon on the front of his notebook, and without prompting he knew what was next. His Sunday school assistant and I praised him for doing so. I bent down and asked him if he liked his notebook, and in typical Casey fashion, he did not look me in the eye. But what he did next was something that amazed and delighted me. Spotting Monica, his assistant in children's church, he took my hand and pulled me into the room behind him. 'Show Monica music!' he said and we went to show Monica his new notebook and 'music.'

"A breakthrough happened that spring day in April. While everything in God's world was growing, Casey was also beginning to grow and learn at church, just like he has been growing and learning at school. And we are growing and learning

After church, Casey was eager

to show his notebook to his

parents.

too; learning what it is like to adapt to a different way of learning, learning what it is like to work with a student with autism, and learning how to celebrate the small steps in life that mean so much."

OTHER DIAGNOSES IN THE AUTISM FAMILY

RETT SYNDROME

Definition: Rett syndrome is a neurological disease which has been found only in girls. They develop typically until six to eighteen months. Then, without explanation, they quickly lose the hand skills they have developed. Other motor skills will deteriorate, their communication goes awry, and they withdraw socially.

Behaviors:
▼ A fixed pattern of hand movements (such as wringing, squeezing, clapping, rubbing) and mouthing can become almost constant while she is awake. This happens after the child has lost hand skills.
▼ Shakiness of the torso and of the limbs when she is upset or agitated.
▼ Severely impaired speech and understanding of language accompanied by severe retardation of intellectual development
▼ Seizures in 80 percent of the girls
▼ Breathing irregularities, which can include hyperventilation or holding her breath

Exceptional Teaching Tips
Access Ministries at McLean Bible Church offers the following practical information to aid you in working with the student with Rett syndrome.
▼ She loves music! So, whatever you plan, include lots of music.
▼ Use pictures or symbols to represent the choices she has. For example, if during quiet time she has a choice of listening to music or having a story read to her, show her a picture of a cassette player with tapes and earphones, and a picture of an adult holding a book. If she is nonverbal, place the pictures far apart from each other and notice where her gaze lingers. Some girls may be able to point to their choice.
▼ Provide plenty of hands-on activities that she enjoys at home and incorporate them into the classroom when appropriate.
▼ Make sure to get her to look at you when you are speaking to her, so that she can understand how happy you are that she is there.
▼ Encourage her with your words and ask her for a hug.

Frequently Asked Questions About Autism

Do kids with autism have mental retardation?
If the answer is based on the scores they get on IQ tests, the answer is yes. About half score below fifty, about 20 percent are between fifty and seventy, and 30 percent over seventy. However, because of the problems they have with communication skills and behaviors, it is not easy to determine the cognitive level of a student with autism.

Aren't some of them brilliant?
A few people with autism are savants. They have some extraordinary skills in music (playing the piano without lessons), drawing (producing pictures freehand that look like they have been traced), mathematics (giving the day of the week months or years in advance when a date is given), or visualization (recalling the end credits of movies and television programs).

What causes autism?
The answer is not easy. There are lots of theories and ideas. A popular one is the shots new-borns receive. Brain damage, genetic influences, or pregnancy complications may cause it. Children born with rubella, or fragile X are likely to develop autism. It is definitely a neurological disorder. The problem is in the brain—in the areas that control speech and language.

Do the symptoms of autism go away?
Not really, but a small group of people with autism can lead normal lives.

ASPERGER'S SYNDROME

Asperger's syndrome, a member of the autism family, is characterized by problems in development of social skills and behaviors. Generally speaking, children with AS function on a higher level than the child with classic autism. Youngsters with AS have normal IQs. Children with autism don't develop language skills or show delays in language. Children with AS use words by the age of two, even though their speech patterns may be a bit bizarre.

Characteristics:
▼ Difficulty interacting with age-mates
▼ Display eccentric behaviors
▼ Often a loner
▼ Preoccupied with an activity (counting objects, watching the same video) for hours
▼ Clumsy and otherwise uncoordinated

- ▼ Limited interests
- ▼ Few facial expressions
- ▼ Excellent rote memory
- ▼ Good at music
- ▼ Verbose on one topic
- ▼ Hand or finger flapping, maybe twisting
- ▼ In his own world
- ▼ Uses pedantic language
- ▼ Good but superficial language
- ▼ Lack of or few gestures
- ▼ Frozen stare

Exceptional Teaching Tips

- ▼ Don't let his behaviors throw you.
- ▼ Respond to him, not his behaviors.
- ▼ Help him understand the routine of the classroom.
- ▼ Remember his receptive language skills are close to typical. He will be aware of what is being said.
- ▼ Let the other children know that he likes to be alone.
- ▼ Permit him to participate in the group on his own timetable.
- ▼ Keep the classroom open and welcoming.
- ▼ Accept his atypical behaviors.

CHILDHOOD DISINTEGRATIVE DISORDER

Childhood disintegrative disorder is similar to autism in that there are impairments in social interaction, communication, and behavior. One of the differences is the time of onset. Children with autism have it from birth and for sure by the time they are three. Children with CDD grow and develop normally for a period of two to ten years. Then they lose their skills in language, social interaction, and adaptive behaviors, as well as motor skills, and control over body functions.

CHAPTER 8

Students With
HEALTH DISORDERS

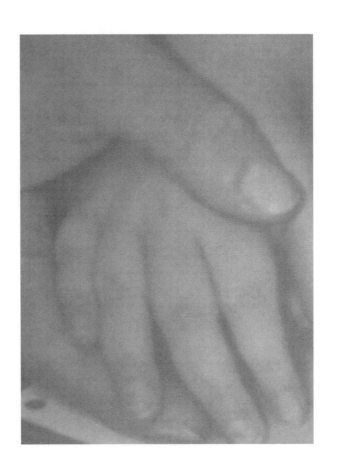

An Exceptional Life Story

The diagnosis was cancer. Jason was nine years old. Two positive people entered his life who helped to make the end of his life special. A teacher for homebound students provided by the school system knew that this bright child had six months remaining in his life. Her lesson plan was simple: Jason will read some of the world's best literature about death. Jason's term project will be to plan his own funeral. The other person was his Sunday schoolteacher who made sure her young student was at peace with his Lord. But she added a dimension. His weakened physical condition made it impossible for him to go to school. So contact with his friends was limited. Miss Jane changed that. Every Thursday after school, the entire class met at Jason's house to do the lesson for the coming Sunday. Some children who were afraid they would "catch" cancer became Jason's most encouraging friends. His parents report that their hugs, give-me-five's, and exchanging of baseball cards will be a lasting memory of their son's last days on earth.

Definition of health disorders

Students with health disorders and students with physical disabilities have something in common: they are restricted in their involvement in typical activities.

The IDEA definition of children with health disorders spotlights the reason the condition requires special education. The student's limited strength, lack of vitality, and reduced alertness will adversely affect his progress in education. The common chronic and acute health problems are listed in the definition: asthma, diabetes, heart problems, sickle cell anemia, and others. Most are discussed in the following paragraphs.

Karen Carter, a former special education student of mine at Milligan College and now a special education teacher in a public school, prepared the material in this section. We have selected diagnoses that are more common and are likely to be a part of a church's education program. If a student with another health disorder appears in your class, his needs will be similar and the suggestions offered here can be adapted for him.

In most cases kids with health disorders can be included in the regular classroom at school and church. The teacher just needs to know a few things to make the environment welcoming and safe.

▼ Always remember it is a *person* you are working with, not an illness. Take time to really get to know his or her individual personality. Because a child doesn't like to be singled out, treat everyone in your class the same.

▼ It is important for everyone who works directly with the child to know about the child's illness and how it impacts his or her participation in church activities. Interview the parents and share the information they give you with the adults who will be working with the child. Discuss the illness, medications, and the possible side effects, emergencies that may arise, and actions to take, foods or activities he needs to avoid, etc. When meeting with workers, stress the importance of confidentiality. Information regarding the student should be shared on a need-to-know basis. Find out where the parents will be in the building so they can be located quickly in case of an emergency. See page 210 for a form for recording this information.

▼ It is a good idea to have two or more adults in the classroom or one available nearby in case of an emergency.

▼ If the student needs to eat a snack (for example, to maintain blood sugar levels), incorporate a snack time into your class time so the child doesn't feel singled out.

▼ Parents can provide suggestions for snacks, and cooperate with treats if they are given advance notice. One mother arranged her son's restricted diet so he could have a cupcake for a party at church. It counted as his sugar intake for the day.

▼ Teach the other students about the child's health disorder. The more they understand about the illness, the more accepting they will be.

▼ Due to his condition, the student may miss church often. Mail him Sunday school papers, send a card signed by the whole class, and keep him informed of special events, etc., so he will continue to feel part of the class.

Students who are dealing with health problems need to be able to participate in typical life experiences. However, you may need to take special precautions to make sure they are safe, and their participation in your class is a positive one. Some general suggestions of ways to help students with allergies and asthma are on the following pages.

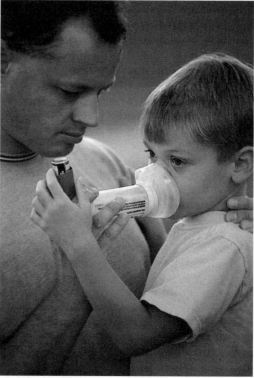

Teachers need to be able to recognize the symptoms of an asthma attack and be prepared to help the student administer his medication.

©2001, Turnrose

ASTHMA

Asthma is a lung disorder. The person has periodic attacks of wheezing, but breathes relatively normally the rest of the time. The wheezing attacks are triggered by a specific allergy-respiratory infection, exercise, cold air, smoke, stress or anxiety, food or drug allergies. During an attack the bronchial tree becomes tight and the lining of the air passages swell, reducing the airflow. Mucus production increases. These attacks can last for minutes or days. The incidence of asthma in children is estimated at one in ten. It can develop at any age, but some children outgrow it. Asthma is treated by avoiding known allergens and using medications to control the symptoms.

Suggestions for helping a child with asthma

▼ Talk to the parents and find out what triggers their child's asthma attacks.

▼ If the child uses an inhaler, become familiar with the dosage and how the child takes it. Monitor the child, but don't give him the medication.

▼ Have a written plan for handling an attack should one occur while the child is in class. Make sure all adults working with the class know the plan. Keep it in a place that can be found quickly (for example, taped on the inside of the cabinet door). The plan should include where the parents can be located in case of an emergency.

ALLERGIES

Allergies are a disorder of the immune system, and many children have them. An allergy is the body's immune system reacting against an outside force it sees as an "invader." Allergies are grouped according to the substance that causes the reaction or the part of the body it affects. These categories include food, skin, respiratory, drug, and insect bites. When the body encounters an allergen, it releases a large amount of histamines, which can create a variety of symptoms including a runny nose, itchy eyes, hives, swelling, vomiting, diarrhea, breathing difficulties, increased heart rate, and possible loss of consciousness. The best treatment for an allergy is to avoid the substance that triggers it. Students may also need to take antihistamines to help counteract symptoms. The most serious type of an allergic reaction is anaphylactic shock. This type of shock can be triggered by any allergen; however, the most common are insect stings, certain foods (like shellfish and peanuts), and certain drug injections. Anaphylactic shock usually is treated by an injection of epinephrine that opens up the airways and blood vessels. Children who are severely allergic to bee stings often carry an emergency kit that has an injection of epinephrine. It is not your responsibility to administer this injection, but it may be necessary to arrange with his parents a plan for doing so in the event the student is stung by a bee while he is with you.

Suggestions for helping a student with an allergy
▼ Know what he is allergic to and how he reacts.
▼ If he has a severe allergy, check your classroom to make sure that allergen is not present.
▼ If he has a food allergy, keep a written list of foods he needs to avoid and a separate list of acceptable snacks.
▼ Make sure an emergency kit with an epinephrine injection is nearby if you are going outdoors with a student who has a bee sting allergy.

When parents tell you that their child is allergic to a specific food, be sure that food isn't provided as a refreshment. During a visit to one children's department, I was impressed with signs announcing the snack for the day. The signs were posted along the hallways, especially in areas where parents dropped off their children. The name of the snack and all of the ingredients were easy to read.

The components of such a plan are easy:
▼ Select five snacks that do not contain any of the ingredients on the "my child is allergic to" list.

TODAY'S SNACK IS HONEY GRAHAM CRACKERS

INGREDIENTS
Enriched Flour (Wheat Flour, Niacin, Reduced Iron, Thiamine Mononitrate, Riboflavin, and Folic Acid), Graham Flour, Water, Sugar, Partially Hydrogenated Soybean Oil, Honey, Dextrose, High Fructose Corn Syrup, Salt, Sodium Bicarbonate, Artificial Flavor, Ammonium Bicarbonate, and Sodium Sulfite.

▼ Serve the same snack each Sunday of the month. For example, serve graham crackers on the first Sunday, and fresh fruit on the fifth Sunday.
▼ Notify the parents of your selections.
▼ Each Sunday, post an enlarged version of the manufacturer's label that lists the ingredients of the snack.

For birthdays and other special celebrations when parents like to bring a treat, suggest that they bring a nonedible gift, like a toy or a coloring book. These two suggestions will make planning easier for you and insure that the student's allergy will not be triggered in your classroom.

AIDS OR HIV

Acquired immunodeficiency syndrome (AIDS) is caused by a virus called human immunodeficiency virus (HIV). HIV is spread through sexual intercourse, sharing of needles, contaminated blood products, or by an infected mother to her newborn. It is important to note that HIV is not spread through

▼ touching, hugging, or shaking hands,
▼ coughing, sneezing, or breathing, and
▼ sharing food, drinks, utensils, crayons, toilets, or common classroom objects.

A child diagnosed with HIV can remain fairly healthy for years, but as the infection progresses, he may feel tired and feverish. As his immune system weakens, AIDS usually develops and a mild illness could become potentially fatal. There is currently no cure for AIDS, but drug treatments are extending the lives of those living with HIV and AIDS. It is possible that you may have a student in your Sunday school class who has AIDS, but you may not know it. Parents have a right to confidentiality and may choose not to disclose this information. They fear their child will be treated differently or not be welcomed by the group. If they inform you that their child has HIV or AIDS, respect their right to privacy and do not disclose it to others without their permission.

Suggestions for helping a student with AIDS or HIV

▼ It is best not to have a meeting to discuss the child's program unless the parents approve.
▼ Ask the parents how advanced the child's illness is.
▼ Teach the other students in the class about HIV and AIDS only if you have parental consent. Reassure them they will not "catch" AIDS by playing, touching, or sharing things with a child who has the disease. It is also important to stress that we should never touch anyone's blood. This is a good precaution to teach everyone to follow even if you don't have a student with AIDS in the class.

▼ Keep gloves and a first aid kit in the classroom to deal with any cuts or injuries that may occur. If an injury occurs and you don't have gloves, instruct the child to hold a paper towel over the wound until you can get gloves.

▼ Use doubled trash bags to dispose of gloves, bandages, paper towels, or other items that have come in contact with blood.

▼ Blood spills should be cleaned using any household disinfectant. A mixture of bleach and water at a dilution of 1:10 to 1:100 is acceptable.

▼ Post the parents' location in the church so that you can find them quickly in case of an emergency.

▼ Your state's health department will have resources that you can use to help your other students understand about HIV and AIDS. You can also contact the CDC National STD/AIDS Hotline:

English: 1-800-342-2437
24 hours, seven days a week

Spanish: 1-800-344-7432
8:00 AM – 2:00 AM EST

TTY: 1-800-243-7889
10:00 AM – 10:00 PM EST, M-F

▼ When handling bodily fluids such as urine, stool, oral or nasal secretions, sweat, tears, and vomit (with no visible blood present), no other special precautions other than hand-washing are necessary.

▼ Because of a child's limited ability to fight infection and disease, common illnesses can be life-threatening to a child with HIV or AIDS. Notify the parents of any outbreak of illness in your class.

CANCER

Two common cancers in children are osteosarcoma and leukemia.

OSTEOSARCOMA

Osteosarcoma is a form of cancer in which cancer cells are found in the bones, usually the shin, thighbone, or shoulder. It can spread to other bones. This form of cancer can occur in children as young as ten. Usually, osteosarcoma is treated with surgery. The child may have to undergo chemotherapy, and in some instances the child is fitted with an artificial limb to replace a missing arm, foot, leg, or hand. A prosthetic device can be made in flesh colors so it appears more natural. Some prostheses have computerized parts that make them more functional for fine motor tasks.

LEUKEMIA

Leukemia is a form of cancer that involves the blood and blood-forming organs. When a person has leukemia, large amounts of abnormal cells render the body unable to fight off infections. The abnormal cells fill the bone marrow, interfering with the production of normal blood cells. These cancer cells also can move to other parts of the body and build up there as well. Leukemia patients generally are treated with chemotherapy, which uses drugs to attack the cancer cells in the bone marrow. In addition, radiation therapy may be required. If the growth of cancer cells cannot be controlled through these therapies, the treatments may be increased. If the increase is not successful, bone marrow transplant may be used. A child undergoing these treatments experiences a variety of side effects including nausea and vomiting, allergic reactions, hair loss, mouth sores and ulcers, jaundice and lethargy, fatigue, and lack of coordination. Changes in physical appearance are common.

Suggestions for helping a student with cancer

▼ Discuss with the child's parents any side effects of medications and/or treatment the child is undergoing. Ask what you need to do if the child becomes ill while in your care. Are there any restrictions on activities?

▼ The child will fear being rejected by his peers. He may also have problems dealing with changes in his physical appearance or his prosthesis. Talk to the parents about ways you can help the child deal with these feelings. Make it easy for the child to talk about his fears.

▼ Be open and honest with your class regarding the child's illness and prosthetic device. Your students will have many questions; answer them as completely as you can. Reassure your students that they cannot get cancer by touching someone who has it.

▼ Celebrate the accomplishments your student makes in learning to use a new prosthetic device. If he feels comfortable, allow him to show off the new skills he has learned and let the rest of your class become cheerleaders for him. You all will have fun together and help the child feel more confident about himself and his accomplishments.

▼ Become familiar with the child's prosthesis and find out what you may need to do if any difficulties arise with it.

▼ Allow the other students to ask questions and answer them as completely as you can. The parents may also be willing to help answer questions. If the child has been absent from class, prepare the other students by informing them of any changes in his appearance before he returns (example, hair loss, swelling, jaundice, etc.).

▼ Discuss death. See page 113 for ideas.

HEART DISORDERS

One in every one hundred babies is born with a congenital heart defect or disease. This estimate accounts for a wide variety of malformations that affect the heart and major vessels. Congenital defects begin in the early part of pregnancy when the heart is forming. Heart disease can occur also in children who have had rheumatic fever or complications from the strep virus. Heart disease can affect the flow of blood through the heart or the heart's ability to function effectively. Children with heart disease may experience difficulty in breathing or have a bluish tint to their skin. Their growth may be slow or abnormal and they may have unusual weight gain. They may also tire easily and feel weak. Some heart defects are minor and can correct themselves while others may require surgery. Children with heart problems may require modifications in their activities because of lack of stamina or endurance. These children may need to take medication.

Suggestions for helping a student with heart disorders

▼ Because of limited stamina and endurance, periods of active play may need to be shortened and rest periods provided as needed. Ask the parents what type and amount of physical activity their child can tolerate.

▼ Because the child may need to eat more often, include a snack time in your class schedule.

▼ Define and explain the child's condition to your class and explain why the child has to limit his physical activity.

▼ Provide some activities that do not require physical exertion.

A child with a lung or heart disorder still wants to play. The teacher must monitor him to guard him from overexertion.

©H. Armstrong Roberts

CYSTIC FIBROSIS

Cystic fibrosis (CF) is an inherited disease that causes the body's glands to produce thick, sticky mucus that affects breathing and digestion. The mucus clogs the lungs and throat and produces a cough. Children with CF have chronic lung infections. CF also affects the pancreas, causing inadequate absorption of nutrients in the intestines, which leads to malnutrition. These children also tend to have large and foul-smelling bowel movements.

Children with CF can live long, healthy lives, but they must follow a strict treatment regimen that may include
▼ physical therapy
▼ exercising to strengthen the heart and lungs
▼ eating healthy
▼ taking enzymes and antibiotics
▼ using a mister to assist with breathing
▼ eating more salt

Suggestions for helping a student with cystic fibrosis
▼ Meet with the parents to find out as much as you can about the child's illness and how it will affect the child's participation in your class.
▼ Be open and honest with your other students about CF. Explain to them what it is, how it affects the student, and that it is not something they can "catch." Invite the parents and child with CF to help you with this lesson and to answer questions.
▼ Ask the parents what to do if the child has an emergency, and keep the parents' location in the church building clearly posted.
▼ Because of the possibility of foul-smelling bowel movements, keep a can of air freshener in the bathroom.
▼ Keep a supply of cough drops in the classroom.

A student with a feeding tube
Feeding tubes are common among children with disabilities. Tubes that place nutrients and fluids directly into the stomach or intestinal tract are used with children who are unable to take in enough calories orally to promote normal growth. Some children are not able to eat or swallow safely because of reflux (food flowing back up from the stomach into the esophagus), aspiration (food inhaled into the lungs), or neurological disorders that affect the development of feeding and swallowing skills. The most common types of feeding tubes are nasogastic and gastrostomy.

Nasogastic (NG) tube—a tube that goes in the nose and through the throat into the stomach. This tube is generally used for short-term or temporary feeding needs.

Gastrostomy (G) tube—a rubber-like tube that goes through the stomach wall directly into the stomach. A gastrostomy tube is used when a long-term feeding option is needed. This tube can be removed if the child's oral intake of food improves enough to meet his nutritional needs.

There are two methods used in tube feeding—bolus and drip. In a bolus feeding, liquids are poured into a large syringe that is inserted into the feeding tube. The feeding usually takes twenty to thirty minutes. A drip-feeding requires a pump that regulates the amount of formula given over a specified period of time. Some children require continuous drip-feedings administered during the day. Other children may receive a drip-feeding during the eight to twelve hours a night they sleep. Commercial formula is generally used for tube feedings and vitamin/mineral supplements may be prescribed also. Fluid levels may need to be increased if the child experiences a fever, vomiting, diarrhea, or during hot weather.

Suggestions for working with a student with a feeding tube
▼ If the child is on a feeding pump, find out how the pump works and what to do if a problem occurs.
▼ Children with a G-tube will have an external "button" where the pump or syringe connects during feedings. Be careful not to pull on the button.
▼ If the child can take food or liquid orally, find out if any precautions need to be taken.

HEMOPHILIA

Hemophilia is an inherited disorder that affects the blood's ability to clot so that a small cut or injury can lead to uncontrolled bleeding. Hemophilia is caused by a deficiency of clotting factor VIII. It affects one out of ten thousand males. Only women carry the trait. Bleeding is the primary symptom of this disorder. Other symptoms include bruising, spontaneous bleeding, bleeding into the joints causing pain and swelling, gastrointestinal tract and urinary tract hemorrhage, and blood in the urine or stool. Administering concentrates of factor VIII at the first sign of bleeding can treat hemophilia. Most people with this disease can live relatively normal and healthy lives.

Suggestions for working with a student with hemophilia
▼ Ask the parents what to do in the event of an uncontrolled bleed. Keep this information posted in the classroom and be sure all adult helpers are aware of the procedures.

▼ Do frequent safety checks in the classroom to look for sharp objects or obstructions that could cause accidents. When children are using scissors or other sharp tools, monitor them carefully.

JUVENILE DIABETES

Juvenile diabetes is a disease of the pancreas that affects the body's ability to produce and utilize insulin. Insulin is the hormone used to convert food into energy. It is a lifelong disease for which there is currently no medical cure. Diabetes is controlled through food, exercise, and insulin. Food causes the glucose (sugar) level in the blood to rise while exercise and insulin cause the glucose level to fall. It is important for students with diabetes to consistently eat at the same time daily. They also need to eat certain types and amounts of food to keep their glucose blood levels balanced. Regular exercise is also important to control the amount of sugar in the blood. Individuals with juvenile diabetes take insulin shots daily. Blood levels must stay balanced or the child may experience hypoglycemia (low blood sugar) or hyperglycemia (high blood sugar).

The symptoms of **hypoglycemia** are crying, confusion, irritability, paleness, shaking, drowsiness, inattention, headaches, nausea, hunger, and weakness. Giving the student a sugary food immediately treats hypoglycemia. Commonly used foods are candy, fruit juice, or nondiet soda. When the reaction subsides, the child needs to eat foods such as milk, bread, or cheese and crackers to prevent a recurrence. **Hyperglycemia** is characterized by excessive thirst and frequent urination.

Suggestions for working with a student with juvenile diabetes
▼ Grant the child's more than usual requests to get a drink or go to the bathroom.
▼ Find out if the child needs to eat a snack during class time. If so, incorporate a class snack time so the child doesn't feel singled out.
▼ Post, for all adults to see, the child's reaction to a sugar imbalance and what steps need to be taken to correct it.
▼ Keep a supply of fast sugars in the room (juice, soda, or candy) and be sure all adults know where the items are located.
▼ Make sure all adults working with the student are aware and informed of the circumstances.
▼ What are appropriate snacks for parties and special events? Generally, children with JD can have popcorn, sugar-free Popsicles, peanuts, fresh vegetables, or cheese.

JUVENILE RHEUMATOID ARTHRITIS

Juvenile rheumatoid arthritis is an autoimmune disease in which the body's white blood cells are unable to tell the difference between healthy cells and tissues and invaders like bacteria and viruses. The immune system then releases harmful chemicals that damage healthy tissues and cause pain and swelling. Juvenile rheumatoid arthritis usually appears between the ages of six months and sixteen years. It begins with joint pain or swelling, and reddened and warm joints.

There are three major types: **polyarticular arthritis** occurs more often in girls and affects five or more joints including the small joints of the hands, knees, hips, ankles, feet, and neck. **Pauciarticular juvenile rheumatoid arthritis** affects four or fewer joints. Its symptoms include pain, stiffness, or swelling of the joints. The knee and wrist are most commonly affected. The child also experiences iridocyclitis or iritis, which is swelling of the iris. **Systemic juvenile rheumatoid arthritis** affects the entire body. The student experiences high fevers and develops a rash. He may also experience enlarging of the spleen and lymph nodes. Eventually, many joints may swell and become stiff and painful.

In about 50 percent of children with juvenile rheumatoid arthritis, the symptoms eventually disappear. Early detection and treatment are the keys to effectively manage and minimize the effects of arthritis. Treatment includes a combination of medication, physical therapy, and exercise. The medication prescribed for the inflammation and pain can have some unpleasant side effects. Exercise is very important to keep the muscles strong and healthy. Safe activities for a student with juvenile arthritis are walking, swimming, and bicycling. Avoid impact sports, which can be hard on weakened joints and bones. Children who receive an early diagnosis and proper treatment can lead normal lives.

Suggestions for helping a student with juvenile rheumatoid arthritis

▼ The more informed you are about what type of arthritis the child has and what joints are affected, the more prepared you will be in working with him.
▼ Allow him to be as independent as possible. If his hands are affected, you may need some adapted scissors or writing utensils. Find out what physical activities are appropriate and safe for the student to participate in.
▼ Learn the side effects the child may experience from his medication and the assistance he may need.

KIDNEY DISEASE

The kidneys remove harmful minerals and chemicals from the blood and produce urine. Without the kidneys, waste products would build up in the blood and damage the body. The category of kidney diseases can include problems from birth defects, obstructions of the urinary tract, and disease of the kidney tissue. These diseases also affect the child's blood pressure and growth and cause anemia. The child's diet needs to be closely monitored. He may feel sick frequently and need to take medications.

Some children may develop chronic kidney failure. Often the symptoms will not present themselves until about 80 percent of the kidney function is lost. When this occurs, two treatment options are available: dialysis and kidney transplant. Side effects from the medications will include weight gain (especially around the face), moodiness, sleep problems, cataracts, and osteoporosis.

Suggestions for helping a student with kidney disease

▼ Discuss with the parents what kind of disease the child has and how it affects him.
▼ Determine the child's dietary restrictions and post them so the other adults are aware. Also find out if he needs to take any medications while he is in your class.
▼ Discuss the possible emergencies and determine plans to deal with each situation.
▼ Find out if the child has any special needs when using the toilet.

SEIZURE DISORDERS

A seizure is caused by unusual electrical activity in the brain. When brain cells send too many impulses to the muscles at the same time, a seizure occurs. The muscles tighten and relax rapidly or stop moving. When the impulses stop, the seizure stops. A seizure disorder may be inherited or can be caused by a traumatic injury to the brain.

There are basically two types of seizures: **tonic-clonic seizures** (old term "grand mal") are characterized by loss of consciousness and shaking. The person may also vomit, drool, urinate, or lose bowel control. When the seizure ends, he will feel tired and will not remember what has happened. During an **absence seizure** (also known as "petit mal"), the person will stop normal activity and get a glazed look, as if daydreaming. He may become unaware of surroundings and may experience jerking movements in one part of his body. When the seizure ends, he often returns to normal activity and may be unaware anything has happened.

Seizures generally occur without warning. Some seizures, however, can be triggered by environmental factors (like video games, excessive heat, or strobe light) or not getting enough sleep. There is a common misconception that during a seizure a person could swallow his tongue and that you should put something in his mouth to keep it from occurring. This is not true. No one can swallow his tongue, and you should not put anything in his mouth during a seizure. About 80 percent of people with seizure disorder are able to control the seizures through medication.

Diane Anderson, director of the Access Ministries at McLean Bible Church in McLean, Virginia, is a good trainer. She provides her teachers with a helpful list of seizures and how to handle each of them. See page 101.

Generally, if a student has a seizure, follow this plan:
▼ Place him on a soft surface (carpet or grass).
▼ Move furniture and other things away to prevent injury.
▼ Lay him on his side to keep him from swallowing vomit.
▼ Do not try to restrain him.
▼ Loosen any tight clothing from around his neck.
▼ Do not put anything in his mouth.
▼ Stay with the student till the seizure is over.
▼ Record the time and symptoms of the seizure.
▼ Allow him to rest after the seizure, if needed.

Suggestions for helping a student with a seizure disorder
▼ Develop an emergency plan with the parents.
▼ If the child has to rest after a seizure, keep a beanbag or blanket and pillow in your room.

Using latex gloves is a wise procedure when dealing with children who have infectious diseases. In this case however, the teacher is simply taking care not to transmit any of her own germs while assisting Jacob with his beverage.

© Jeff Greenburg/Photri, Inc.

How to Handle a Seizure

Petit mal or absence seizures:

These seizures can be a blank stare, beginning and ending abruptly, lasting only a few seconds, most common in children. They may be accompanied by rapid blinking, and some chewing movement of the mouth. The person is unaware of what's going on during the seizure, but quickly returns to full awareness once it has stopped.

What to do? No first aid is necessary, but if this is the first one that has been noticed, ask the family about it and inform the rest of the staff in your program.

Simple partial seizures:

Jerking may begin in one area of the body—arm, leg, or face—and can't be stopped, but the person stays awake and is aware of what is going on. The jerking sometimes spreads to other parts of the body, becoming a convulsive seizure; or the person may experience a seizure that is not apparent to anyone else. These usually consist of unexplained fear, sadness, anger, or joy. The person may report smelling bad odors and complain of feeling sick.

What to do? No first aid, but follow the basic approach of taking care of a person who is having a seizure.

Complex partial or temporal lobe seizures:

This seizure usually starts with a blank stare, followed by chewing and random activity. The person appears unaware of surroundings, may seem dazed, and mumble. He may be unresponsive to surroundings, may pick at clothing, or try to remove clothes, or may run or appear afraid. This seizure will develop into a pattern that looks much the same every time it happens. While it lasts only a few minutes, the post-seizure confusion can last longer. There will be no memory of the seizure.

What to do? Be calm and reassuring. Keep the person away from hazards. Stay with him until full awareness has returned.

Atonic seizures or drop attacks:

A child may suddenly collapse and fall. After a few seconds he will recover, regain consciousness, and be able to stand up and walk again.

What to do? No first aid is necessary unless there has been an injury in the fall.

Myoclonic seizures:

These seizures are sudden, brief, massive muscle jerks that involve the entire body.

What to do? No first aid is necessary, but inform the family when one occurs.

Infantile spasms:

These spasms are clusters of quick, sudden movements that start between the age of three months and two years. If the person is sitting up, the head will fall forward and the arms will flex forward. If lying down, the knees will be drawn up, with arms and head flexed forward as if he is reaching for support.

What to do? No first aid is needed, but tell the family. The doctor is probably having them keep a record.

▼ Keep a change of clothes in your room in case the child wets himself during the seizure.

▼ Find out if the child has any dietary restrictions.

▼ Talk to the class about seizures. Explain to them the characteristics, and what to expect if a classmate has a seizure. Be sure to tell them they cannot catch a seizure disorder and that their friend is not in any pain during a seizure. The first time they see a seizure it will be scary, but the more informed they are the easier it will be to understand and react.

SICKLE CELL ANEMIA

Sickle cell anemia is an inherited disease that affects the red blood cells. Normal red blood cells are soft and round and travel easily through blood vessels. Sickle cells, however, are stiff with a curved shape that makes them look like the sickle tool used by farmers, hence the name. Because of their hard, curved edges, they do not flow well through blood vessels and so will clog areas and prevent blood flow. The brain, heart, and kidneys can be affected by this loss of blood flow. The body attacks these sickle cells but cannot produce new blood cells fast enough to replace them, which leads to anemia or low red blood cell levels.

When a blockage caused by the sickle cells occurs, the child may experience pain in his chest, stomach, or bones. Pain from these blockages can be alleviated with medication. The low number of red blood cells causes the child to feel tired more easily and get infections more often than other children. He may also grow more slowly than his peers and have a diminished appetite. Jaundice and frequent urination are other common symptoms. Children under the age of two may experience swelling and pain in their hands and feet. Sickle cell anemia mainly occurs in people of African-American heritage. Some people who have ancestors from countries around the Mediterranean Sea (Greece, Italy, and Saudi Arabia) have sickle cell genes as well. Children with sickle cell anemia take penicillin to help prevent infections. They also take folic acid to help the body produce new red blood cells. Transfusions can be used to increase the level of healthy blood cells in the body.

Suggestions for helping a student with sickle cell anemia

▼ Ask the parents for a clear description of how a blockage of sickle cell anemia affects their child. How does the child respond? What signs do you need to look for and what actions do you take? Make sure this information is posted in the classroom and all teachers are aware.

▼ These kids need to eat healthful foods—ask the parents for a list of appropriate snacks. They also need to drink lots of water and get plenty of rest.

▼ Children with sickle cell anemia can play games and sports, but they need to avoid becoming too hot, cold, or tired.

▼ Explain this disease to your class and how it affects their classmate. Also make them aware of how the child may act if a blockage of cells should occur.

▼ If the child complains of aches or has a fever, let the parents know right away. The fever may be a sign of an infection, and the pain may be the beginning of a blockage of cells in the blood vessels.

Concluding this section on health disorders is a good place to suggest that you set up a health plan and put into place some universal precautions. The chart on the following page will give some ideas.

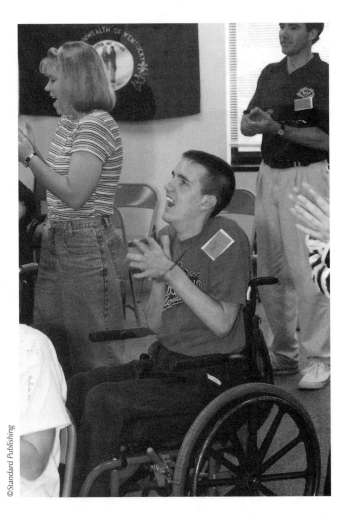

Music helps all of us express our love for God. Bart and Corey have that much in common with each other, and with believers around the world.

Health and Safety Policies

The disturbing and traumatic rise of physical and sexual abuse of children and youth, and the fear of infectious disease has claimed the attention of our society. The following policies reflect our commitment to provide protective care of all children, youth, and volunteers who participate in the special needs ministry. Never promise a child or parent that you won't tell. Adult volunteers should report immediately any behaviors that seem abusive or inappropriate to the coordinator.

Two Adult Minimum Policy

Our goal is for each class to be staffed by a minimum of two adults. If only one adult is present, another adult must be recruited to work for the class period or the class must be combined with another until a second adult is found.

Bathroom and Diapering Procedures

No one is ever to be alone with a child when changing his or her diaper or escorting the child to the rest room. Please always find another volunteer to assist you or take some other students who may also need to go to the rest room.

Use of Latex Gloves

▼ Volunteers must use a new pair of gloves for each child and each instance.
▼ Volunteers must dispose of gloves after each use and never reuse them.
▼ Required when handling blood.
▼ Required when handling any body fluid (i.e., vomit, urine, diarrhea).
▼ Required each time you change a diaper.

Washing Hands

Proper handwashing is the best defense against exposure to diseases. Thoroughly wash hands in the following instances:
▼ After accompanying a child to the bathroom.
▼ After assisting a child in wiping his or her nose.
▼ After contact with blood or any other body fluid.
▼ After using the bathroom.
▼ After contact with your own nasal secretions.
▼ Before preparing or handling food.

Accidents

Volunteers will use Accident Report Forms (sample found on page 209) to report any accidents, minor or major, and treatment applied. Volunteers will clean up immediately in the event of an accident, using disinfectant for wiping up all spills or soiling by blood, urine, or feces. Volunteers also must report any spills on rugs or any other surface that cannot be easily cleaned up.

Health of Volunteer

Any volunteer with a temporary contagious illness is requested to refrain from serving until well.

Clean Toys

Volunteers will attempt to keep toys from being shared, particularly those put in someone's mouth. When someone is seen putting a toy in his mouth, volunteers must wash the toy with disinfectant before the toy is returned to general toy containers. The disinfectant will consist of one part bleach to ten parts water.

CHAPTER 9

Students With
PHYSICAL DISABILITIES

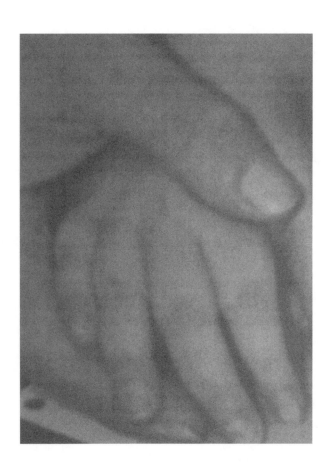

If a student in your class has a physical disability, the most important word to guide your understanding of him is "restriction." He may not walk as well, run as fast, jump as high, or be able to participate in the regular outdoor activities. *Removing barriers* is the most important factor in creating a good environment for him. The child with a physical disability needs to know that he is in a safe, easy-to-move-around-in place.

Definition of physical disabilities
IDEA uses "orthopedic impairment" rather than "physical disabilities" to describe this group of children. The law also stresses that the impairment must interfere with the child's education. Three kinds of impairments are recognized: impairments resulting from **congenital anomalies** (a missing limb), from **disease** (polio), and from **other causes** (cerebral palsy).

An Exceptional Life Story
Carl is a delightful eight-year-old. He has a broad smile. He uses a wheelchair for most of the day. When he is at home, he uses a walker on a limited basis. For example, he will use his walker to get from his place at the dining table to a chair in the den. He understands everything that is said to him. His speech is about 50 percent intelligible. Even though he is messy, he can feed himself using a spoon. If the rest room is accessible, he can take care of his elimination needs. He does well in a regular classroom at school. He is a good reader and enjoys math. He receives speech therapy two days a week. A physical therapist works with him once a week. An occupational therapist is helping him improve his eating skills. He is proud of his baseball card collection. While he enjoys video games, his favorite activity is watching football on television. Attending the Boy Scout meeting is the highlight of his week. He has cerebral palsy.

©Standard Publishing

Cody has mild CP. His buddy Tim stays with him on an as-needed basis to provide Cody with a helping hand. Tim's primary role is as friend, to ensure that Cody knows that church is a warm and accepting place to be.

CEREBRAL PALSY

Cerebral palsy is likely the most widely known physical disability. Cerebral palsy is a disorder caused by damage to the brain. "Cerebral" means the damage is in the areas of the brain that control movement and posture. "Palsy" refers to muscle weakness and inability to make voluntary movements. Cerebral palsy often causes multiple disabilities. The person may have mental retardation, seizures, communication problems, vision and hearing impairments, and physical limitations. Depending on the site of the damage and the extent of it, the cerebral palsy may be mild or severe. Most often the cause of CP occurs during pregnancy, labor, or just after birth. It cannot be cured. It is not progressive. It cannot be caught.

Children with cerebral palsy are often described by the motor impairment they display:

▼ **Spastic** is the most common type. It accounts for about 60 percent of cerebral palsy. The muscles are tight and contracted. The result is difficulty moving.

▼ **Athetoid** is the second most common type. The child experiences constant, uncontrolled movement of the arms, legs, head, and eyes.

▼ **Ataxic** causes the child to have a poor sense of balance. The condition causes frequent falls and an unsteady gait.

▼ **Rigidity** is characterized by very tight muscles that are resistant to any attempt to make them function.

▼ **Tremor** causes shaking that the child can't control, often interfering with coordination.

Arrange your classroom

so that the student in a wheelchair

or the student who uses a walker

has room to get around.

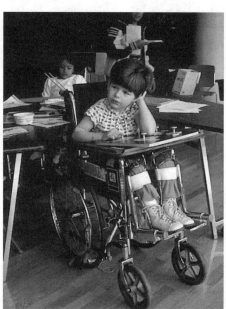

©Tom McCarthy/Photri, Inc.

Useful information

Children with CP receive lots of attention from physical, speech, and occupational therapists. They often wear braces, use walkers and canes, and have wheelchairs. Neurologists and orthopedists are familiar doctors to them. Medications may be used to reduce tension and control problems associated with damage to the nerves. Technology helps the person with cerebral palsy control his environments.

Knowing the common characteristics of the person with cerebral palsy will add to your confidence level. Not every person with cerebral palsy will have every characteristic; however, you will note some of the following behaviors in the student in your classroom.

▼ More than half have mental retardation
▼ Rigidity; the muscles are tight and resist moving
▼ Difficulty with speech and conveying ideas
▼ Unsteady gait and lack of balance
▼ Tremors; the muscles shake
▼ Frustration caused by limitations and attitude of peers
▼ Lack of coordination
▼ Learning deficits caused by perceptual problems
▼ Poor muscle control
▼ Poor concentration
▼ Seizures
▼ Paralysis ("hemi" means one side of the body, "quad" means all four limbs)
▼ Poor use of hands

You can help the student with cerebral palsy feel comfortable in your classroom if you create a positive learning environment. The following ideas will be useful in developing a welcoming classroom:
▼ The student may need help with the basic physical functions, depending on the severity of the cerebral palsy.
▼ Vary the methods of teaching.
▼ Be a model for the other students, showing them how to feel comfortable with their fellow student.
▼ Give the student enough room. A wheelchair, walkers, a seizure, and awkwardness require space.
▼ Learn the student's stress and fatigue limit.
▼ Know what the student can do, more than what he can't do.
▼ Familiarize yourself with any special equipment and its care.
▼ Train student peers to help.
▼ Obtain special supplies, such as double-handed scissors, which allow an assistant to hold the scissors the same time as the student.
▼ Use a lot of tactile activities involving materials such as finger paint, sand, water, and shaving cream.
▼ Involve the student in musical activities using homemade band instruments.
▼ When the cerebral palsy or other physical disability makes speaking difficult,

learn to understand as much as you can. If the intelligibility of the speech is so poor that quick responses cannot be made, devise a method for a "yes" and "no" response. For example, have the student hold up one finger if the answer is yes and two if the answer is no. This approach can be developed according to the physical capabilities of your student. Or, create a language board with a picture for water, toilet, and food. Teach the student to point to the appropriate response.

▼ Give the student an opportunity to demonstrate his gifts and talents to the entire class.

While these ideas will help create a pleasant classroom, dealing with the student in a caring, one-on-one, friendly manner is equally important. Become comfortable with the information on page 111 in order to make the student feel at home.

SPINA BIFIDA

An Exceptional Life Story

Sally is a cute little blond. She wears braces on both legs and uses crutches. She has some problems keeping up with her third-grade classmates. Much of her delay is caused by her frequent absences for surgery and therapy. She takes a medication to control seizures. She has a shunt, an implanted device that prevents spinal fluid from collecting in her brain. Pleasant and chatty, Sally enjoys being with her friends and listening to music. At birth, Sally was diagnosed with myelomeningocele, the most common and the most severe of the three types of spina bifida.

Three types of spina bifida

Spina bifida occulta is the one that causes the least amount of problems. The vertebral column doesn't close properly. Surgery to close the opening is often all that is necessary to correct this type.

Meningocele is a lot like occulta. The difference is that there is a hole in the vertebrae. Skin pouches out but there is no nerve tissue involved. Again, surgery usually takes care of the problem.

The student in your classroom will most likely have Sally's diagnosis, **myelomeningocele**. In her case, there was nerve tissue involved in the pouching skin. Even with surgery, Sally is paralyzed from where the opening is on her back and below. She is incontinent.

Assisting the Student with Physical Disabilities
The Key: Work with the person, not the disability

1. Know what to do during a seizure (For more detailed information see page 101.)

▼ Above all else, stay calm.

▼ Reassure the other students in the classroom that everything will be fine.

▼ Allow or assist the child to reach the floor so he will not be hurt.

▼ Let the seizure run its course, don't try to stop it.

▼ Cover or stand in front of an object that could injure him if he hit it.

▼ Place the child on his side to assist good breathing and allow saliva to drain.

▼ Do not put anything (your fingers included) in the child's mouth.

▼ Give the child time to rest after the seizure.

▼ Reorient him.

2. Adapt the classroom to the child's special needs

▼ Think through what to do in an emergency with a child in a wheelchair or one who can't manage to get out on his own or quickly.

▼ Don't alarm the other children by telling them about the plan, but discuss it with the other staff members. The procedure may never be used, but you will have peace of mind knowing you have thought it through.

▼ Be sure the classroom has good paths of travel for a student in a chair, on crutches, or on a walker.

▼ Provide storage of the student's equipment, aids, and other stuff.

▼ A useful piece of equipment is an office chair with arms and casters. It provides a quick and easy way to move a child.

▼ Put materials the child needs within easy reach.

▼ Allow some extra time for the child to move around.

3. Watch your language.

One of the difficulties in helping children use and understand the importance of a kinder and gentler way of speaking is the language from the King James Version of the Bible. "Crippled" and "deaf and dumb" are two of the most notable examples. More current translations are not always free of insensitive language either. When I read a passage of Scripture that contains a word or phrase that can be expressed more kindly, I do it. For example, instead of reading "a paraplegic," I say, "a man with a physical disability." The nonreaders don't know the difference. If a reader asks a question about the change, you have a good opportunity to teach a language lesson.

Some special language reminders

▼ "Paraplegia" means legs only

▼ "Hemiplegia" means one half of the body

▼ "Quadriplegia" means all four limbs

▼ "Double hemiplegia" means the arms are more involved than the legs

▼ "Crippled" is not a good word to describe physical disability. It sounds harsh, especially when the person is present.

Useful for working with students with spina bifida:

▼ There may be some cognitive problems.

▼ In some cases there may be hydrocephalus (spinal fluid on the brain). If so, learning problems probably will be present.

▼ Bladder and bowel difficulties are a symptom. (Accidents can happen. Your student, in most cases, will have been trained to deal with both bladder and bowel functions.)

▼ The higher the opening on the spine, the more serious the problems.

Tips for making the classroom comfortable:

▼ Ask the parents about specific medical problems.

▼ Be sure the floor is safe for crutches and other orthopedic devices (not slippery).

▼ Know if the student has a history of pressure sores.

▼ Learn how to position the child in order to prevent sores.

▼ Become familiar with the child's wheelchair.

▼ Know how to maintain a catheter.

▼ Anticipate and plan for incontinence.

▼ Inform fellow classmates about the problem in order to create a positive environment for the student with spina bifida.

▼ Promote an atmosphere that will allow the student to build a positive self-image.

MUSCULAR DYSTROPHY

An Exceptional Life Story

When Tommy was in preschool, his teacher reported to his parents that he fell a lot on the playground. Because he had lots of spills at home, his parents observed their son more carefully. His father's nonmedical assessment, "Tommy's feet don't work," started the evaluation process that resulted in the medical diagnosis of Duchenne muscular dystrophy.

Now as a ten-year-old he is in a regular class at school and receives physical therapy and occupational therapy. The goal of physical therapy is to keep his muscles as strong as possible. He uses a wheelchair. Because he is losing the functional use of his hands and arms, the occupational therapist's goal is to make him as active as possible. The medical team who cares for Tommy has told his parents that their son will die in his late teens or early twenties. When Tommy was diagnosed and his mother learned that she carried the recessive gene that caused her son's condition, she and her husband decided not to have more children. So, the idea of losing their only son and child is an extremely sad one. Nonetheless, they keep themselves and Tommy involved the routines of life. Picnics, basketball games, and church activities are a part of his weekly schedule.

Muscular dystrophy is the term used to refer to nine hereditary diseases that destroy muscle tissue. The variety in the disease is determined by the age of the person, the muscles involved, and how rapidly it develops. Generally speaking, MD is a progressive muscle weakness. It occurs when the fat cells and connective tissue replace good muscle tissue. It starts in the feet and moves up the body. Frequent falling is a symptom that gets the child to the doctor and a diagnosis.

When the heart and diaphragm muscles deteriorate, respiratory problems occur. The type Tommy has, Duchenne's, is the most common one. It happens one in every thirty-five hundred births. Onset of Duchenne's muscular dystrophy is usually between two and six years of age. MD usually affects only boys. Life expectancy is late teens to early twenties.

There is no cure for MD. It can be prevented by genetic counseling. The help the person receives is physical therapy to keep him as independent as possible, and devices (most use wheelchairs by the time they are fourteen).

Exceptional Teaching Tips
▼ Involve the student in as many activities as he can manage physically.
▼ Stress his strengths.
▼ Do not pull him by his arms. This may cause dislocation.
▼ Prepare other students for the reality of their friend's early death.
▼ Find out what his gross and fine motor skills are. Is he able to use a pencil, scissors, glue bottle, crayons?
▼ Will he need help in the rest room?
▼ Ask parents if there are any learning or cognitive problems.
▼ The student with MD will experience difficulties with balance. Stress with your other students the need to be careful around him.

Discussing death
The child with muscular dystrophy in your class has a shortened life span. He knows it, and his friends in the class will soon know it. So, provide them with some good information on how to deal with it.

First, find out from the family what the child knows and how he has reacted to the information.

Second, explain that death is a part of life.

Third, use some passages of Scripture that describe death.

Fourth, don't gloss over the concept of death.

Fifth, use literal, direct terms to describe death.

▼ "Sleep," to a child, means the person can wake up.

▼ "Passed away" doesn't say what happened. It is an adult way of not saying "died."

▼ "We lost our friend" conveys to the child, "We might find him."

▼ "Up in Heaven" could mean "If I get high enough I can see him."

Sixth, be honest and reassuring to the child.

▼ "I really don't know the answer to your question, but I have thought about that too," is an honest answer.

▼ "I feel sad too. I will miss talking with him about his cat," is an answer to assist the child in expressing his own feelings.

Seventh, use the experience to stress the importance of being ready for eternal life.

DWARFISM

Dwarfism is a general term for medical conditions that result in short stature. The Little People of America (LPA) define dwarfism as an adult height of four feet, ten inches or shorter. It is the result of the disproportionate growth of the skeleton. In most cases it is the result of genetics. Most children with dwarfism have parents of average height. In the main, they have normal IQs, can expect a normal life span, and enjoy good health. While there is debate about the issue, the Americans with Disabilities Act recognizes dwarfism as a disability. "Dwarf," "little person," "LP," and "person of short stature" are OK terms. "Midget" is not.

Exceptional Teaching Tips

▼ Make sure the student can reach everything.

▼ Use a step stool to reach something, even if you don't need the extra height. It keeps the student from feeling alone.

An Exceptional Life Story

Danette Baker, a delightful friend of mine who lives in Spokane, Washington, has a rare missing enzyme disorder called **Mucopolysaccharidosis** (MPS), or **Morquio's syndrome**. She is three feet, two inches tall. Though small in body, she is large in spirit. She exudes excitement about life, people, and God. At age sixteen she attended a Little People of America Convention and realized that she could lead a normal life as an adult. When I asked her how Sunday schoolteachers should relate to children of small stature, she responded: "Children who are noticeably different should be treated just like other children. They need to be mainstreamed as much as possible and their difference needs to be pointed out as little as possible. On the other hand, their difference needs to be acknowledged, and they need to have the opportunity to talk about this difference. They need to know that something is wrong with their bodies and not them."

BRITTLE BONE DISEASE (OSTEOGENESIS IMPERFECTA)

OI is a genetic disorder that results in abnormal, fragile bones. It is caused when the body makes either too little or poor quality type 1 collagen (the protein that "scaffolds" the bones). It is a physical problem, not a cognitive one. The condition causes the bones to break easily. There are four types. The student in your classroom is likely a Type I. It is the most common and mildest form and the child has a good life expectancy. Type II is the most severe due to respiratory problems. The child dies at birth or shortly thereafter. A child with Type III has a shortened life expectancy, and few live to be adults. A child with Type IV has a good life expectancy.

The common symptoms that will vary are
▼ bones that fracture
▼ deformed extremities
▼ short stature
▼ loose joints
▼ low muscle tone
▼ whites of the eyes have a gray, blue, or purple cast
▼ triangular face
▼ spinal curvature
▼ brittle teeth
▼ hearing loss
▼ barrel-shaped rib cage
▼ respiratory problems

Exceptional Teaching Tips
▼ Your approach to the child should not be, "If I touch him, he will break."
▼ Never pull, push, or bend an arm or leg.
▼ When handling a baby, lift by putting one hand under the buttocks and legs, and the other under the shoulders, neck, and head.
▼ If diaper-changing is a part of the routine, ask the mother or caregiver to show you the procedure to follow.
▼ Remember: Touch is important to babies and children, so don't refrain from touching out of fear of breaking a bone; just be as gentle as possible. The bones will break, no matter how careful you are.
▼ Listen to the instructions of the parents. They have developed good ways of handling the child.

AMPUTATIONS

There are two types of amputations:

Congenital
▼ Within the first month after conception the arm and leg buds appear. If the process does not continue, the child is said to be born with an amputation.
▼ These youngsters adapt easier to their prosthetic devices than do children who have acquired amputations.
▼ Causes are often attributed to drugs and genetics.

Acquired
▼ After birth, amputations may result from injuries or surgical procedures.
▼ One cause is cancer. It is discussed on page ninety-two.

Exceptional Teaching Tips
▼ Be direct with the class about any prosthetic device the student is using.
▼ Be sure you know how to take care of the device if something happens.
▼ Encourage the children to ask questions. Parents look forward to answering questions with their child.

The building code information on the next page is adapted from *Accessible Building Design* published by the Eastern Paralyzed Veterans Association, phone number: 718-803-3782. Local building code advisors can provide the information you should adhere to.

The teacher has so successfully captured

the attention of these students that neither

Charles nor any of his classmates are aware

of his helmet.

©H. Armstrong Roberts

Assessing Accessibility

A curb ramp
▼ must be a minimum of 3' wide
▼ maximum 1" rise per each 1' distance

A wheelchair ramp
▼ must have handrails 32" high
▼ be a minimum of 3' wide
▼ should be covered with non-slip surface
▼ each 50" rise must have level rest platform 5' length minimum
▼ changes in direction must have a 5' x 5' platform of clear floor space

Handrails
▼ should be 1 $\frac{1}{4}$"–1 $\frac{1}{2}$" diameter
▼ should be mounted 30"–34" from floor
▼ must be at least 1 $\frac{1}{2}$" away from wall
▼ railing should be extended 1' beyond top and bottom of ramp

Vestibules
▼ should have at least 4' of clear space whenever there is a series of doors.
▼ The force required to open the vestibule doors can be up to 8 $\frac{1}{2}$ pounds.
▼ If there is a threshold at a door, it must be beveled and no higher than $\frac{1}{2}$".

Doors
▼ 2'–8' of clear floor space
▼ minimum width of 2' 10" (3' desirable)
▼ threshold should be $\frac{1}{2}$" high, maximum
▼ Handle must be easy to use and not require tight grasping or twisting. (This eliminates the use of the traditional doorknob.)
▼ Force needed to push or pull door open cannot exceed 5 pounds.

Rest rooms
▼ 60" wheelchair turning diameter

▼ Showers must have clear floor space, grab bars, hand-held shower heads, and transfer seats.

Toilets
▼ should be mounted 14"–19" high
▼ grab bars should be 33"–36" high
▼ paper dispensers should be 19" from floor.
▼ toilet stalls 56"x 60" minimum (59"x 60" if toilet is floor mounted)

Sinks
▼ should be mounted between 29"–34" high
▼ 6 $\frac{1}{2}$" depth minimum
▼ bottom edge of mirror should be no higher than 40" from the floor
▼ faucets should be easy to use
▼ soap and towel dispensers should be within reach of wheelchair
▼ clear floor space must be provided at each fixture

Drinking fountains
▼ must have clear knee space
▼ spouts and controls may not be higher than 36"
▼ controls must be operable with one hand and not require tight grasp
▼ controls should be located near the front

Hallways
▼ 36" minimum to allow space for one wheelchair
▼ 48" minimum to allow space for one wheelchair and one ambulatory person
▼ 60" minimum to allow space for two wheelchairs

Elevators
▼ 51" x 68" minimum
▼ controls must be 35"–48" from floor
▼ Doors must remain open long enough for a wheelchair user to enter or leave.

Physical Disability Etiquette

The following information will help you feel more at ease when working with situations faced by students with physical disabilities.

How to handle a wheelchair
▼ The wheelchair is an extension of the student. Call no more attention to the chair than to eyeglasses or a hearing aid.
▼ Don't lean on, hang onto, or prop your feet on the chair.
▼ Before you push, be sure the person is secure and the brake is off.
▼ When entering an elevator, back the chair in so that the person is not left facing the rear wall.
▼ If your conversation is going to last more than a few minutes, position yourself on eye level. Don't lean over in a patronizing manner, but sit down. This is not only polite, it's a great way to prevent a sore neck.

Shaking hands
▼ The general rule is to share the same social courtesies with the person with a disability as with those without disabilities.
▼ If the person uses a hook, has a missing right hand, or whatever makes shaking hands awkward, extend your hand anyway. The person will use his left hand, touch your shoulder, or do whatever he does when greeting others.
▼ Ask the person what he wants you to do. For example, I have a friend whose paralysis starts at his shoulders. After we shook hands the first time, he asked me to put my hand on his shoulder. He has feeling there, so my greeting means more.

When a student wears a helmet
The purpose of a protective helmet is to prevent further injury if the person falls.
▼ Ask your friend who wears one if he would like to remove it while seated.
▼ Be sure he puts the helmet on before standing.
▼ Leave it on if the parents tell you to do so.

When the student uses an electronic device
The world of technology has made many devices available to our friends. If your friend uses a language board or other electronic device:
▼ Learn as much about it as you can, especially how to install batteries.
▼ The device is an extension of the person and should not have undue attention called to it.
▼ If the device is used for communication, be patient. It takes time.

CHAPTER 10

Students Who Are
HEARING IMPAIRED
OR DEAF

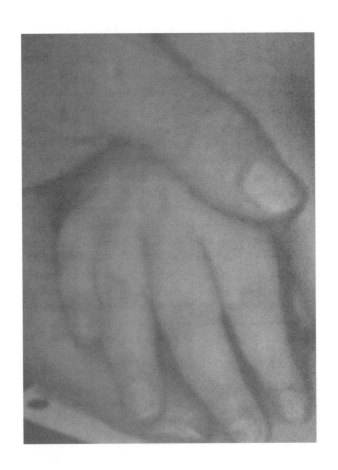

If you have a student with a hearing loss in your class, you need to know just how much he is hearing. Consider these terms:

▼ **Hearing impairment** is used to describe any level of hearing loss, from mild to severe.

▼ **Normal hearing** suggests that the student hears at a level to understand speech without the use of amplification.

▼ **Hard-of-hearing** means that the student has a hearing loss but can use his hearing to understand speech—often with a hearing aid. Even though the student has a hearing loss, he still develops his language and speech skills through the auditory track.

▼ **Deaf** means that the student cannot use hearing to understand speech. Even with amplification, the child depends on vision for learning and communicating.

Definition of hearing impairment

IDEA recognizes two categories: deafness and hearing impairment. The student who is deaf does not use hearing to understand speech, even with amplification. While the deaf student may pick up sounds through residual hearing, he relies on his sight for learning and communicating.

The student with a hearing impairment, which may range from mild to severe, still depends on the auditory channel for learning and communicating; however, the hearing loss adversely affects his education.

Types of losses

A student in your classroom will likely have one of these terms on an audiologist's report: conductive, sensorineural, or mixed.

Conductive hearing loss is caused by whatever keeps the sound from moving along the ear canal into the middle ear where it can be processed by the brain. The loss

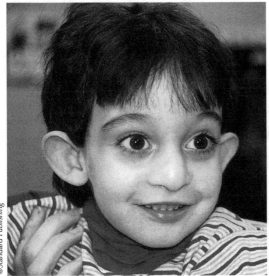

It is easy to see that Michael, who has multiple medical needs and is deaf, enjoys coming to church!

121

can be reversed medically. In children, this loss is often caused by fluid in the middle ear.

Sensorineural hearing loss is caused by damage to the inner ear or the auditory nerve or both. The result is that some sounds can be heard and some cannot. It is a more serious loss than a conductive one and cannot be corrected medically. Mumps, head trauma, and meningitis are some of the causes.

Mixed hearing loss means that conductive and sensorineural difficulties are present.

Central auditory hearing loss means the student has problems understanding language even though the hearing tests show that the hearing levels are normal.

The degree of the hearing loss

Normal hearing means that the student can detect the full range of sounds at a soft conversation level. Hearing is tested by frequency (hertz) and intensity (decibels). The intensity or loudness is measured by decibels, named in honor of Alexander Graham Bell, and indicated by the symbol dB. The following list gives the generally accepted levels of hearing loss and how a child's communication skills are altered.

Slight hearing loss: 15 to 25 dB below normal

This student will hear the vowel sounds without any problem, but may miss a few consonants. He will do OK with keeping up with the conversation. He may use a hearing aid and get speech therapy. His teacher will want to be sure he is seated for his best hearing potential.

Mild hearing loss: 26 to 55 dB below normal

Speech spoken normally will be fine; however, faint speech will present problems. This student misses a lot of what goes on in the classroom, especially if several students are talking. Some of his classmates may not know he has a hearing problem. A hearing aid will help.

Rhonda is teaching sign language to a group of volunteers who will then serve as worship service interpreters and as buddies for students who are deaf.

©Standard Publishing

Moderate hearing loss: 56 to 70 dB below normal

Understanding normal speech will be hard. If the child is in a large group, he will miss a lot of what is said. If the speaker is directly in front of the child, five or six feet away, he will likely get the message. There are more speech problems in this student. His voice will lack resonance. Even with the speaker talking loudly, the student will have problems understanding. Following the conversation in your classroom will be almost impossible.

Severe hearing loss: 71 to 90 dB below normal

This child will not be able to speak in a manner that strangers understand. His hearing is very limited. He may be able to hear a shrill noise, like a burglar alarm. The slamming of a door would get his attention. If the speaker is talking loudly close to the student's ear, he may hear the sound. He will hear voices only if the person speaking is less than one foot away. He uses a hearing aid, but its helpfulness is not clear. He hears vowel sounds but few consonants. He communicates with signs and some speech. He *really* looks at the person who is talking to him.

Profound hearing loss: 91 dB or more below normal

Any student with this level of hearing loss will communicate by signing, by lip reading, or by writing. He probably will have little or no speech that can be understood. If he participates in the class he will need an interpreter. His hearing aid helps him be aware of loud sounds. American Sign Language is his primary language.

In addition to being aware of the communication skills of your student, you also need to understand his other abilities.

▼ **Intelligence:** Students with hearing impairments have the same cognitive abilities as those students without hearing impairments. The difference, if any, is a problem of language development, not cognitive development. Many people with hearing losses resent being thought of as having mental retardation.

▼ **Academics:** Students with hearing impairments will have trouble with reading (more than the other subjects). Writing is simple, short, and rudimentary. Arithmetic can be deficient.

▼ **Social Skills:** While there are examples to the contrary, the social skills of most people with hearing impairments are less mature than those of their hearing peers. The lack of information from the auditory channel is the culprit.

Exceptional Teaching Tips

▼ Speak normally. Talking louder really doesn't help.

▼ Be sure that the light is accenting your face, not glaring in the child's face.

▼ Face the child when speaking to him.

▼ Be sure you have the child's attention.

▼ Use a lot of gestures. However, make them meaningful, not just a lot of random movements of the hands.

▼ Repeat important words. You may even want to write them. (An overhead projector is good for such purposes.)

▼ Control as much extraneous noise as possible.

▼ Adding carpet will help with the sound problem.

▼ Use a lot of visual aids.

▼ Be sure the child is seated where he can see you and the rest of the class. A circle arrangement is a good idea.

▼ Learn enough signs from American Sign Language (ASL) to make the child feel that you want to communicate with him.

▼ Teach the class members some signs as well. They will love it!

▼ Encourage the child to ask questions.

▼ Summarize the material.

▼ Repeat comments or questions from other students in the class.

Special note: If the child has an interpreter, talk to the child not to the interpreter. The conversation should be directed to the child. For example, do not say to the interpreter: "Ask Sean if he wants to go play on the playground." Say, "Sean, do you want to go play on the playground?" The interpreter will translate.

Another special note: Keep extra batteries handy, of a size to fit the child's hearing aid. Batteries tend to die at the most inopportune times.

To make the child who is deaf/hearing impaired comfortable in children's programs or the church service, see the information on the next page.

This teacher is demonstrating good technique by getting the attention of the child she wishes to speak to, and by clarifying the directions for him.

©Dennis MacDonald/Photri, Inc.

Teaching Students Who Are Hearing Impaired

Don't	Do
▼ Refer to persons who are deaf as "deaf and dumb" or "deaf-mute."	▼ Learn sign language (even a little bit will be helpful).
▼ Place your hands in front of your mouth when communicating with a person who reads lips.	▼ If you do not know sign language, find some other way of communicating (i.e., pointing, writing on paper, etc.).
▼ Turn away from the person who is deaf while you are talking.	▼ Include the person who is deaf in the conversation when a hearing person joins in.
▼ Talk down to an adult who is deaf.	▼ Help the person who is deaf feel comfortable at social events. Introduce him to your hearing friends.
▼ Stare.	▼ Hire or train a sign language interpreter for services and classes.
▼ Become discouraged if you have trouble learning sign language. Try to go for a few simple phrases like "Good morning," "How are you today?" "May I help you with anything?" Take it slowly.	▼ Use visual stimulation in the church service.
	▼ Use extra bass in worship time. Persons who are deaf can feel the vibrations.
▼ Be afraid to ask the person who is signing to slow down. There will be times when you also need to talk slowly, as when you are communicating with a person who reads lips.	▼ Involve the person who is deaf in the service. He can pass out bulletins, collect offering, read Scripture, etc.
	▼ When communicating with a person who reads lips, speak clearly in a normal tone of voice and don't rush.
	▼ Encourage hearing children to include children who are deaf in other activities of the church (mission trips, camp, sports, etc.).
	▼ Offer a sign language class for church members who are interested.

125

CHAPTER 11

Students Who Are
VISUALLY IMPAIRED
OR BLIND

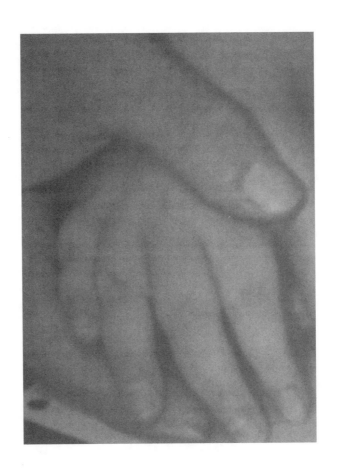

Two Exceptional Life Stories

Janie, trailing the back of her fingertips deftly down the corridor wall, stops for a sip of water from the fountain, locates her Sunday school room door, and enters with a bounce. She returns the cheerful greetings of her classmates with an eager grin, locates a chair, and opens her brailled Bible school manual to today's lesson. Janie is blind.

Down the hall Brian has entered his preschool class ahead of his mother, his eyes brightening through thick frames as he recognizes his buddies. They join hands as they scamper toward the table to explore the activity for the day. Brian is visually limited and, like Janie, at home in his Bible school, where he and his friends are learning about the wonderful stories of the life of Jesus.

A special word about language

While "people first" language is the rule of the day in other disabilities (Adam has autism), this is not the case with the blind. The National Federation of the Blind discourages euphemisms such as "visually challenged," "people with blindness," "people who are blind," and "sightless." The membership of that organization voted in July of 1993 to say "blind" when the person can't see and to say, "visually impaired" to distinguish between those with no eyesight and those having some. So, be comfortable in using "blind" and "visually impaired."

IDEA directs educators to classify students with visual limitations by how much they use their vision and/or how much they use the sense of touch for learning.

▼ **Totally blind** means the student has no real input from vision. Instead he uses touch and hearing to learn about his world.

▼ **Functionally blind** means the student uses braille for reading and writing. He also depends on his limited vision to walk through a classroom or to sort objects by color.

▼ **Low vision** refers to people who can read print, even though they use magnifiers or large print. Some can read print and braille. They might be legally blind but still be able to employ vision in learning.

Janie relies on senses other than vision to obtain information, requires adapted methods, materials, and equipment for learning, and is considered educationally blind. She uses braille and/or listening as the main avenue for learning.

Brian uses corrective lenses and requires adaptive methods, materials, and/or equipment in order to use his remaining sight as a channel for learning. He is considered visually limited. He reads large print or uses a magnifier.

Note: Some of the material in this section is adapted from "Seeing With the Heart" by Marsha B. Uselton, in *Reaching Out to Special People* (Standard Publishing, 1989, out of print).

The following terms will be useful in understanding the student with vision problems:

Legally blind refers to people whose visual acuity, measured in both eyes while wearing correctives lenses, is 20/200 or whose visual field is no more than 20 degrees.

Visual field or **field of vision** is the area the person sees when he is looking straight ahead.

Canes are often used to assist in moving around.

Guide dogs are used when the person reaches the teen years.

Braille is the system of six raised dots used by the blind person to read and write. It is much slower than reading print. A good average for a braille reader is one hundred words per minute. Since children are introduced to braille in the first grade, it takes a while for the readers to be proficient. They use both a brailler and a slate and stylus. The brailler is a hand-operated machine with six keys that relate to each dot in the braille cell. The paper is embossed with the braille code. The slate and stylus creates the code as well. While slower, it is lighter and easier to transport.

Myopia is nearsightedness.

Hyperopia is farsightedness.

Astigmatism is distorted or blurred vision.

Ross studies the board intently in his eagerness to learn. He was born with mental retardation and is visually impaired, but he is one of those guys who is willing to try harder.

©Standard Publishing

Strabismus means the eyes do not fixate and track together.

Nystagmus is the rapid, back and forth, involuntary movement of the eyes.

Amblyopia might cause a person to wear a patch over his stronger eye. The vision in the weaker eye is less from the lack of use, not disease.

Photophobia is sensitivity to light.

Some helpful information

Most blind people have some level of light or object perception and field defects (not seeing on a certain side, seeing only peripherally, or having blind spots). You will want to know how the child uses his remaining sight.

Ask his parents:
▼ Does his sight help him avoid obstacles when he moves around?
▼ Does it assist in locating dropped objects?
▼ Does his use of vision change with lighting, fatigue, or emotional state?

Encourage your student to use his remaining vision.
▼ He can't use it up.
▼ Close eye-work may cause irritability, fatigue, or headache, but it will not further impair his sight.

Your blind student will feel the full range of emotions, just as any other student. Blindness does not automatically bring with it feelings of insecurity or sadness. He will be both gloomy and cheerful, fearful and confident.

Your student will not be any more spiritual or musical, or gifted in any way beyond a sighted student, except as all of us have different gifts.

The way others treat him will have a lot to do with the way his personality develops. Encourage your sighted students to get to know their new friend and include him in all of their activities. The experience will enrich them.

There will be some differences to consider.
▼ He may be behind educationally. It takes a long time to learn braille.
▼ It has taken him longer to learn tasks others pick up casually by visual imitation.
▼ Because of a better use of memory than his sighted age-mates, he may be on age-level.
▼ He may lack understanding of certain concepts in cases where touch cannot replace vision, for example, color, perception of distance, the height of a building or the depth of a hole—with serious consequences!

Some practical matters

The following ideas will enable you to include the student with vision problems more completely in your class.

- ▼ Explain the materials to be used in the lesson.
- ▼ Know the size print he uses and print parts of the lesson for him to hold.
- ▼ Enlarge workbook pages or other parts of the lesson materials.
- ▼ Make copies as dark as possible. Use a marker to make lines darker.
- ▼ Avoid using colored ink and paper; it messes up the contrast.
- ▼ If the student uses braille, find someone in your town who can braille parts of lessons for him.
- ▼ Seat the student so he can see you.
- ▼ Don't use glossy-surfaced materials.
- ▼ Vary instruction methods.
- ▼ Use lessons with auditory and tactile components.
- ▼ Use objects instead of pictures whenever possible.

The classroom should be a pleasant place for the student with vision problems. Encourage your student to

- ▼ express his feelings toward his classmates,
- ▼ develop relationships with his friends,
- ▼ express his needs.

Suggestions for creating a safer classroom

- ▼ Leave doors fully opened or fully closed, and drawers closed so students don't run into them.
- ▼ Let the child visit the classroom when the rest of the students aren't there. Describe where the furniture is, where the water fountain is, where the rest room is, etc.
- ▼ Describe the location of things, especially after rearranging the classroom.
- ▼ Be sure there is enough room to store the student's "stuff." Braille materials take up a lot of room.

©Standard Publishing

Lakin, who is visually impaired, is trying to cooperate. Here she tells her buddy Judy, "If I had my reading device, I could see that!"

Exceptional Teaching Tips

▼ It is perfectly OK to use words such as "see," "look," and "blind." Do not worry about struggling to find substitutes (blind people "look" with their fingers).

▼ A visually impaired child's behavior needs guiding just as any child's. Set reasonable standards of behavior.

▼ We tend to talk more loudly than usual when communicating with a blind individual. It doesn't help.

▼ Do not talk to others about the person, no matter how young, as if he were not there. Whispering, gesturing, or "sneaking by with things" in the presence of a person who cannot see is definitely out!

▼ Physical contact is an important way to share warmth and acceptance, especially with young children. Encourage independence whenever possible, and help classmates learn not to be too helpful.

▼ Introduce yourself by name until the blind person knows your voice and encourage classmates to do so. Speaking to him by name will let him be sure when he is being addressed. Let him know when you move away, so he is not left talking to air.

▼ Instead of drawing attention to any repetitive mannerisms a blind student may have, keep him involved in an activity to alleviate the problem. A quiet touch to the head may remind him to hold his head up or stop rocking behavior. (Arrange these touch signals with the student privately.)

▼ Check your own feelings—be sensitive to his needs, but get any tears out of your eyes and understand that pity is only damaging. Your attitude will be an example to the others in the class.

▼ Help a child develop a realistic view of himself, with the expectation of success but not perfection. Avoid regarding every accomplishment as amazing, but help him feel that a full, normal life is a realistic expectation.

▼ Remember that this person is more like other people than different. Treat him naturally. Relax and enjoy the opportunity!

See chart, "Integrating the Visually Disabled Into Worship and Sunday School," page 134.

A buddy system

A buddy system is a great idea for students with any disability, but it is especially good for students who are visually impaired. A classmate can be a helpful buddy to a student with a visual impairment, with the goal of having the student begin work as independently as possible. The buddy may quietly narrate a video, lead the student through a new activity, and provide mobility assistance when needed. Monitor the arrangement to see that it is not burdensome to either party. Arranging opportunities for a visually impaired student to be a helper to a classmate also can be a rewarding experience.

Integrating the Visually Disabled Into Worship and Sunday School

Seat him in the best light. However, do not make him look directly into the light, and avoid glare.

Use dark green or black chalkboard with large-sized chalk or broad strokes of regular-sized chalk for the most contrast. Keep the board clean at all times and write in large letters.

Cover all shiny surfaces (such as a glass cupboard) to cut down the glare in the classroom.

When you use visual aids be sure to use the maximum contrast. Move from one scene to the next slowly so that the visually limited student has time to focus on the scene.

Do spot checks. Ask students to point out certain objects on a video or overhead. You will obtain information about:
- effectiveness of material
- attention of students
- listening skills
- student's vocabulary

Don't raise your voice when talking to the student.

Avoid babying the student. However, remember that physical contact is important to communicate warmth, caring, and acceptance.

To enhance mobility:
- A friend with sight can help the person with visual disabilities in unfamiliar territory. A sighted guide should allow the person with visual disabilities to take his arm and walk a half step behind the guide. When the guide moves his arm from the outward position to the backward position, the person with visual disabilities will know to step behind the guide in order to walk in a narrow hall or through a doorway.
- The student with visual disabilities may brush his fingertips along the wall a few inches in front of his body to move around an unfamiliar area. This technique is called wall-trailing.
- Using sound waves bouncing off objects in the person's path is called "facial vision." The person with visual disabilities will cross himself with his arms to protect him from running into objects.
- The sighted person can describe the room by using the face of a clock. One example is to say, "The table is at one o'clock; the bookcase is at three o'clock."

Use reading materials adapted for learners with visual limitations. Such materials include braille, large print, and recorded materials.

People learn best by doing. Help the person with visual disabilities in learning:
- Sensory stimulation is talking about textures of various objects while touching them. This technique will help students associate words with textures. The same is true with tasting.
- Singing helps to express emotions. When your class is involved in an active song, step behind the child with visual disabilities and help him move his arms and legs to the music.
- When preparing art activities, darken the lines of the picture to be colored and choose high-contrasting colors for the students to use. When choosing pictures to show, select those that have strong color contrast and a minimum of background clutter. Use uncoated paper to reduce glare.

Plan some recreation activities that your student can be involved in. The student with the visual disability needs as much exercise as any other student. Some of these activities include:
- Beep ball—these balls are available from organizations serving the visually impaired or, you can make your own by tying a jingle bell to a balloon. Use these balls for any game requiring a ball.
- Ring Run—A child with visual disabilities can run along a horizontally stretched rope with a key ring or hoop around it. When he holds onto the ring, he will be guided by the rope.
- Students with visual disabilities can play on playground equipment. They can also participate in field trips and games that have been slightly modified.

Prepare the sighted children in your classroom for the introduction of a visually disabled student into the class. Talk about how everyone is different. Ignorance about visual disability is often the reason for hesitation to become involved. Educate your students with a lesson or two about the encounters Jesus had with people with visual disabilities.

ALBINISM

A person with albinism lacks pigmentation in the eyes, skin, and hair. The results are impairments in visual acuity, nystagmus, photophobia, problems with hearing, and mild problems with blood clotting. Albinism is an inherited condition. One in every seventeen thousand people has some type of the condition. Children with albinism develop normally. It doesn't cause developmental delay or mental retardation. If either is present, it has another cause. The life span is normal.

Here are some ways to help the student with albinism:
▼ Openly discuss the child's condition with the class.
▼ Make the classroom a welcoming place to be.
▼ If the child wears sunglasses, give everyone a pair to welcome him. That says "You're OK, we're OK."
▼ You may have to insist that the child use his glasses.
▼ Don't be concerned about the head tilt.
▼ Understand that it may be routine for him to hold objects close to his face.
▼ Use materials that offer the maximum contrast in color.
▼ Put some of the materials in large print for the child.
▼ Keep a magnifying glass handy.
▼ Be sure the lighting is good.
▼ If an outdoor activity is planned, think about how you will protect the child from the sun.

A word about braille

Braille is difficult to learn because from a six-dot cell the reader must memorize 263 configurations, including the alphabet, numbers, and shortened forms of words. Obtain some braille materials for your church library. The following vendors can help:

American Bible Society
National Distribution Dept.
1865 Broadway
New York, NY 10023
800-32-BIBLE
Info@americanbible.org
www.americanbible.org

American Foundation for the Blind
15 W 16th Street
New York, NY 10011
800-AFB-LINE
abinfo@afb.net
www.afb.org

American Printing House for the Blind
PO Box 6085
Louisville, KY 40206
800-223-1839
www.aph.org

Braille Bible Foundation
PO Box 948307
Maitland, FL 32794-8307
(800)-766-9080
www.careministries.org/bbf.html

**National Library Service for the Blind
and Physically Handicapped**
Washington, DC 20542
(Library Of Congress) http://www.loc.gov/nls

Recording for the Blind and Dyselexic
20 Roszel Rd.
Princeton, NJ 08540
609-452-0606
www.rfbd.org

Internet sources:
Christian Resources for Blind Persons: http://www.jci.net/~crs/
Christian Record Services: http://www.jci.net/~crs/
Church Accessibility for the Blind and Disabled:
http://www.ft-wayne.in.us/health/church_accessibility/1231fb.html

CHAPTER 12

Students Who Are
DEAF-BLIND

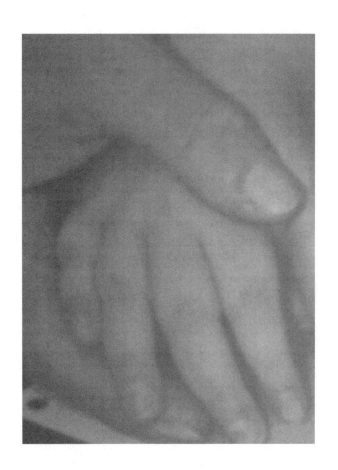

If you have a student in your class who is deaf-blind, he is a part of the least common disability. He is also a part of a varied group. While they all need some level of support, they are not all considered to have a severe disability. Over 90 percent of children who are deaf-blind have some functional vision and/or hearing. In addition, they will have the full range of intelligence. The level of cognitive ability, amount of vision, amount of hearing, and the extent of training will determine the student's level of functioning. Some, like the well-known Helen Keller, will have above-average intelligence and be high achievers. The child's problem is from birth (congenital) or it happened after birth (acquired).

Two common causes are rubella (German measles) and Usher syndrome. Rubella is a common cause. If a pregnant woman had contact with German measles during the first trimester, the baby is likely to have vision and auditory problems, and possibly cerebral palsy. An inoculation controls the condition. Usher syndrome is a genetic disorder caused when both parents carry the condition but do not have it. Their offspring will be born deaf and gradually lose sight.

Definition

Deaf-blindness is defined by IDEA as a combination of hearing and vision problems that cause "such severe communication and other developmental and learning needs that the persons cannot be appropriately educated in special education programs solely for children and youth with hearing impairments, visual impairments, or severe disabilities, without supplementary assistance to address their educational needs due to these dual, concurrent disabilities."

Be aware that the person who is deaf-blind often develops self-stimulatory behaviors. There may be some stereotyped behaviors like head-rocking, finger-snapping, and hand-flapping. He may appear unresponsive or passive. This behavior is likely caused by the person's efforts to satisfy his need for motor-sensory stimulation.

Method of communicating

The teacher who is including a student who is deaf-blind (also called dual sensory impairment) must know the student's method of communicating. The method will be determined by the level of sensory loss, his understanding of language, and his ability to use the method. Some methods follow:

▼ Tactile signing (the person who is deaf-blind places his hands over the hands of the person who is his communication partner)
▼ Deaf-blind manual alphabet finger-spelling (information is given in the palm and fingers of the deaf-blind person)
▼ Print on palm (complete words are spelled with the index finger by using the shape of the letters)

The previous methods are for the person who has no functional use of the visual or the auditory. If the person has some vision, he uses sign language, note-taking, and lip-reading. This information points to the fact that for a student who is deaf-blind to be included in a class, he must have a person who can communicate what is going on and what is being taught. Work with the family to find a partner. Understanding the students method of communication will help the process.

Exceptional Teaching Tips

▼ Learn the student's preferred method of communication.
▼ Allow time to communicate with this student.
▼ The student should be seated with his back to the light source in the room.
▼ Explain the layout of the room to the student. Get rid of clutter. Tell the student where items are located. Don't move them.
▼ Keep background noise in the room to a minimum.
▼ Use the tactile sense to teach. The person who is deaf-blind depends on touch to understand his world. Use an object to define what is happening. For example, when asking the student if he wants a drink, hand him a glass.
▼ Define the setting. Before the class starts, tell the student who else is present today, what the schedule is, that someone is wearing a cast because of a broken arm, and any information that we assume everyone else notices.
▼ Provide the student with nonverbal, nonvisual cues. "Joey laughed." "Jill put her head on the desk." This is especially helpful during group discussions.
▼ Develop a tactile schedule represented by objects.
▼ Use objects to provide a choice.
▼ Touch your student to signal communication or that a new event is starting.
▼ Develop a tactile sign for who you are, and who the members of the class are. When you present yourself to the deaf-blind student, guide his hand to a ring, watch, a bearded chin, etc. Class members will have fun deciding what will represent them.

Helpful technology

The three types of technology listed below suggest that there is a world of assistive devices for people who are both deaf and blind. The cost of this equipment is often a drawback to owning it.

The student may use or have access to several tools available to him.
▼ **TeleBraille III** allows a person who is deaf-blind and a person using a TDD (Telecommunications Device for the Deaf) to talk on the telephone. Typed information is translated and displayed as braille.
▼ **Brailletalk** is a little plastic box that has the braille letters and symbols with the English letters and symbols. The communication partner helps the student find the appropriate letter/symbol and creates the message.
▼ **Braille Lite** is a portable notetaker and reader. The text can be inserted on a disk and the user receives the message through braille that is transmitted via pinpoints.

An essential, valuable resource for information about people who are deaf-blind is The Helen Keller National Center, 111 Middle Neck Road, Sands Point, NY 11050. Telephone: 516-944-8900.

CHAPTER 13

Students With
SEVERE AND MULTIPLE DISABILITIES

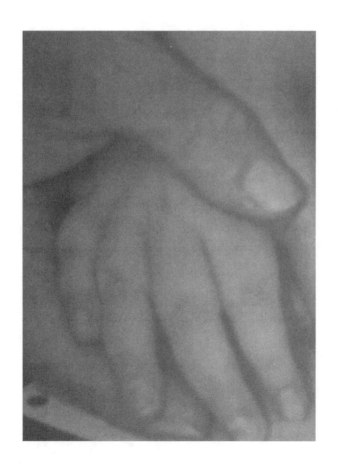

If you have a student with a severe disability in your class, you have a blessing in the wings. In working with these children I have found that locked away in the depths of their souls is a wonderful treasure that only the persistent are able to uncover and enjoy.

The use of the terms "severe" and "multiple" can be confusing. Often people believe that children in this category have mental retardation and don't understand what is happening in their environment. While many of these children do have serious cognitive problems, some of them are really bright. They just don't have a good way to express their thoughts.

For example, one of the most severely disabled persons I know doesn't walk or talk and depends on an assistant for all of his self-care needs, including eating and bathing. However, in school he was always on grade level in reading. He is one of my e-mail buddies. He paints with a device fastened to his head with a pointer (called a head wand). While still in school, he held a one-man show of masks at a local art gallery. His e-mail (written with the head wand, one letter at a time) reveals an understanding of language, his world, his needs, and who he is.

As I have worked with people with severe disabilities, I have often received amazing blessings. Granted, the blessings did not occur in some cases, nor were they often or consistent, but they occurred often enough to let me know that under all of the definitions was a human being who wanted to be cared about.

IDEA definition
The IDEA definition will help sort out the child you may have in your class. "The term 'children with severe disabilities' refers to children with disabilities who, because of the intensity of their physical, mental, or emotional problems, need highly specialized education, social, psychological, and medical services in

Little Daniel has multiple problems including seizure disorder and cerebral palsy, but he seems content to have Rosemary assist him during music time.

order to maximize their full potential for useful and meaningful participation in society and for self-fulfillment. The term includes those children with disabilities of emotional disturbance (including schizophrenia), autism, severe and profound mental retardation, and those who have two or more serious disabilities such as deaf-blindness, mental retardation and blindness, and cerebral palsy and deafness. Children with severe disabilities may experience severe speech, language, and/or perceptual-cognitive deprivations, and evidence abnormal behaviors such as failure to respond to pronounced social stimuli, self-mutilation, self-stimulation, manifestation of intense and prolonged temper tantrums, the absence of rudimentary forms of verbal control, and may also have intensely fragile physiological conditions."

After reviewing the definition, note the types of students included:
▼ Children with intense problems who require extra, specialized service to reach any potential. Specific disabilities include
  – Autism
  – Severe or profound mental retardation
  – Severe emotional impairments
▼ Two or more disabilities together
  – Cerebral palsy and deafness
  – Mental retardation and blindness
▼ Children with the absence of basic communication skills, behavior control, and the presence of fragile medical conditions.

In order to achieve the peak of who they can be, they will need lots of assistance. Even after it is given, they will never be totally independent. Knowing the four levels of support the student needs will help you understand how to work with him better.
▼ **Intermittent** means the supports are given as needed.
▼ **Limited** refers to a support being provided for a specific amount of time. For example, during the time the student needs the service of a speech therapist.
▼ **Extensive** suggests regular intervention, in some environments, with time not being an issue. Requires more staff.
▼ **Pervasive** supports are constant, high intensity, essential, and use several staff people.

Characteristics of students with severe/multiple disabilities
▼ Most don't read, write, or do academics.
▼ It is difficult to tell an IQ level because of their limited use of language.
▼ They have poor memory.
▼ May appear dazed, drowsy, or agitated.
▼ May cry or make constant noise.
▼ Behaviors are not age-appropriate.
▼ Most have poor social skills, although some react pleasantly to people in their environment.

▼ Most will not walk and will use a wheelchair or other mode to move about. A few may be taught to walk with assistance.

▼ Some will have tight muscles; others will have underdeveloped and floppy muscles.

▼ Some may not be able to hold up their heads.

▼ They will have poor usage of their hands.

▼ Vision and hearing problems are common.

▼ Speech and language skills are limited.

▼ Some use communication boards and computers.

▼ Their health is often fragile. They may require catheterization, tube-feeding, and respiratory ventilation.

▼ Seizures, both mild and severe, are common.

Exceptional Teaching Tips

▼ Remember, there is a jewel in there!

▼ Don't be bothered by the lack of response.

▼ Work out a way to communicate with the student. For example, two eye blinks mean "yes" and one means "no." One lift of the eyebrow means "I want a drink."

▼ Find a strength that the other students in the class can appreciate in their friend.

▼ Before talking with the student, be sure you have his attention.

▼ Let him be involved by doing a chore in the class—even if it's a small one.

▼ Assist the student in making friends with class members.

▼ Know how to handle any device he may be using to make his life easier. A language board may be a computerized machine that has some basic words built into it and he touches the word he wants. It could be a homemade, laminated cardboard on which his mother has pasted a few key words that he points to to express his needs. Whatever the equipment—a head wand or a hearing aid—ask parents to show you how it works.

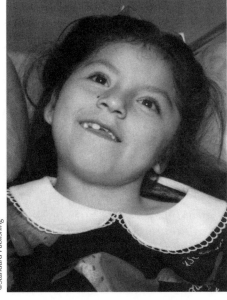

This loving and happy child is Maria. She has

CP, MR, and visual and hearing problems.

She's one of those jewels who will add sparkle

to the lives of those who work with her.

▼ Help his classmates respect the devices. They are not toys.

▼ Talk to the student's parents and other teachers, and find out what works and what does not work with this student.

▼ Take "ownership" of the student so that he feels like a real member of the class. Don't be overwhelmed by his needs.

▼ Develop a picture and work schedule for daily activities. Use this to prepare the student for transitions to new activities.

▼ Relax and know that whatever level of understanding about Jesus' love gets through is valuable.

Children with severe disabilities often have difficulty feeding themselves. If your student does, ask the parents which foods cause choking. If it is necessary for you or an assistant to feed the student, follow the parents' instructions carefully. Be clear on the position he should assume, the size of the portion, and how far into the mouth the food should be presented to him.

A great idea

Hope House, a part of Southwest Christian Hospice, serves the needs of families and children with progressive life-threatening illnesses and severe disabilities. Located in Union City, Georgia, services are both home and center based. Using a home-based approach, Yvonne Strickland started a wonderful ministry to children who can't leave their homes. She explains what she does:

"The Homebound Children's Sunday School Ministry provides in-home Sunday school for children who are unable to attend church because of long-term illnesses, or short-term recovery after an accident or severe illness. This program grew out of my work as a respite provider at the Hope House Children's Respite Hospice. A family we served expressed concern for their child's spiritual growth.

"The parents had tried to do Sunday school themselves for their child, but with all the extra physical care their child needed, it wasn't the same. I am the Sunday school division director for younger children (first and second grades) at Harp's Crossing Baptist Church. When I told my staff about this idea they were very supportive, offering literature and supplies.

"Catherine Richards, my first pupil and the one who got me started, is on a ventilator. Cognitively, she is on par with her age-mates, but physically she is very limited. I do a full Sunday school session with her each week consisting of Bible study, games, crafts, music, and prayer. Music is her favorite activity. While a Christian CD is playing, I sing and move her hands and arms to the music. This activity always brings out a big smile. Recently I have started bringing a child or two her age from church with me. She enjoys having other children there and the children I bring are blessed to be ministering to another child.

"Since each child I teach is different, I gear each session to that child's needs and abilities. For a child with severe brain damage, I might just sing, "Jesus Loves Me" to him and say a prayer. Most of our children have different degrees of cerebral palsy so I go with what works in each case. I have found most all children react to music. A child with autism who has difficulty in group settings can benefit from this program—working one on one, and occasionally joining his regular class at church.

"Homebound Sunday school doesn't have to be on Sunday. We joke about our Monday school, Tuesday school, etc. Also, it doesn't have to be at home. You could apply this concept to a child during a long hospital stay.

"Parents are grateful for the spiritual training, love, and care their children are receiving. While I am there they also get a break (respite time) to go to church, shop, or do whatever is on their schedule."

An Exceptional Life Story

Tim has severe disablities resulting from surgery to remove a brain tumor. He does not walk or talk. He reclines on a beanbag in a fetal position. His parents needed Tim to attend Sunday school so that they could attend Sunday school and church together instead of swapping off on alternate Sundays. The following plan emerged to develop a class for Tim.

We decided to train eight assistants from two colleges and the congregation. In the presence of the volunteers, I asked the parents, "What caused the problem? How does Tim communicate? Does he have seizures? Does he see well? Does he hear? Does he have allergies? What else do you want us to know about Tim?"

We established the goal of letting Tim know he is loved and valuable. The assistants were encouraged to touch and give Tim eye contact.

We decided that until Tim was familiar with the church setting, he would have his own room. The room would reflect his chronological age, and he would use a beanbag. Tim would have the opportunity of hearing a lesson in which a Bible story would be read or told. We would play music for him, and keep a log each week. A refreshment would be available. Because Tim has to be fed, only a beverage would be offered.

The staff handled Tim's seizures. When he had a petit mal seizure, the workers recorded it in the log. An emergency plan was available. Because Tim would have to be carried out of the church building in the case of an emergency, an evacuation plan was in place. The results were great!
▼ Tim learns the meaning of Bible stories.
▼ He enjoys the friendship of eight volunteers.
▼ He takes walks and counts cars, parking meters, and animals.

▼ He sits in a wheelchair instead of a beanbag.
▼ He communicates by nodding.
▼ He responds to music.
▼ His parents attend church and Sunday school together.

A most useful organization:
TASH (formerly Association for Persons With Severe Disabilities)
29 West Susquehanna Avenue, Suite 210
Baltimore, MD 21204
410-828-8274
TTD: 410-828-1306
E-mail: info@tash.org
Web: www.tash.org
Fax: 410-828-6706
M-F 9:00 am to 5:00 pm EST

CHAPTER 14

Students Who Are
FUNCTIONALLY
DELAYED

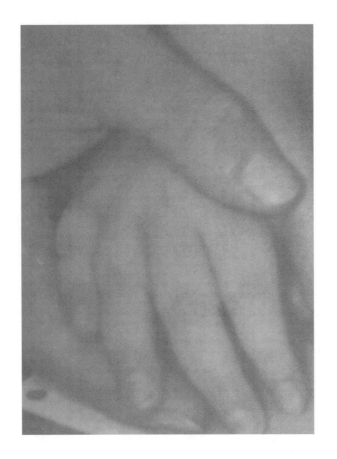

An Exceptional Life Story

Kathy lives with her parents and younger brother in a rural community. She is a pleasant young lady who enjoys helping her parents work in the garden. Because she likes little kids, she volunteers two afternoons a week for her church's day-care program. A freshman in high school, she receives special education services. Daily she goes to the resource teacher who helps her with reading and math. She is really doing well. Her reading level has gone up two grades. "Someday, math will be better," she reports. "Functionally delayed" is the classification that gets her the assistance she needs.

IDEA definition

"A child who has or develops a continuing disability in intellectual functioning and achievement, which significantly impairs the ability to think and/or act in a regular school program, but who is functioning socially at or near a level appropriate to his/her chronological age."

Kathy is an on-target example of the reason this category was added. She does well socially. She gets along well with her peers. She enjoys regular activities. Testing shows that she doesn't have mental retardation, and she doesn't fit the criterion for learning disabilities.

There are many youngsters like Kathy out there. They do OK, but something is just a little different. If you have such a student in your class, there isn't a lot of changing that you need to do to include him or her. The biggest problem is the attitude that youngsters this age display toward their friends who are different.

Two suggestions will help you help your students.

First, be proactive in welcoming Kathy.
▼ Encourage a couple of the class members to sit with her.
▼ Find out something special about her and tell the class. "Our new member collects teddy bears. She has forty!"
▼ If Kathy feels comfortable doing so, have her talk about her interests.

Second, help the students to understand the disability. Help them think through their attitudes and actions toward their friends who are different. Try these activities. (The following material is from *Tips for Teachers, Teens,* Standard Publishing.)

▼ **My Buddy:** Train teenagers to be buddies to their peers who have disabilities. Suggest specific ways to help: pushing a wheelchair, turning pages, assisting in feeding, or simply sitting with their friend during class or worship.

▼ **In His Steps:** Study the Bible to see how Jesus interacted with people with disabilities. Let students list His responses (i.e., compassion, acceptance, touch). Look at Psalm 139; Matthew 25:31-40; and Luke 14:7-24.

▼ **Career Day:** Hold a session in which teens will be introduced to the many careers open to them in Christian service with the disabled and their families. Have information—or representatives—available from colleges that prepare students for disability-related vocations.

▼ **Watch Me:** Model Christ-like responses to persons with disabilities. Teens will learn by your example, so it is extremely important for teachers and other adults to lead in displaying patience, compassion, and tolerance.

▼ **Up Close and Personal:** Invite an adult with a disability to visit your class or group. After a brief, informal presentation, allow students to ask questions.

▼ **Volunteer:** Encourage teens to connect with community agencies that serve the disabled. Invite a representative of the Special Olympics (see page 153) to share with your students how they could be involved as coaches or assistants. Suggest that students volunteer for special programs offered through the local parks and recreation department. Support and encourage students as they reach out in this way.

▼ **Be Prepared:** Take time to prepare nondisabled students when you are aware that a teen with a disability will be joining your class. Give details about their new friend's disability, any specialized equipment he uses, and how they can be a friend.

▼ **Ask:** If you have a student with a disability and are unsure of his or her needs, ask.

▼ **Walk a Mile in My Shoes:** Use simulation activities to help sensitize students to the daily struggles faced by those with disabilities. Lead a session in which each of your students has to perform a series of daily tasks while blindfolded, in a wheelchair, or physically limited in some other way. Spend time debriefing after this session.

This medal-winning Olympian

expresses the joy of victory!

©Ankenbrand

Special Olympics

Another way teens can develop a better attitude toward their classmates who have disabilities is to participate in the Special Olympics.

Created by Eunice Kennedy Shriver in 1963 as a summer camp for children and adults with mental retardation, the Special Olympics have become one of the best-known recreational events for persons with disabilities. The games are open to children and adults with disabilities. The oath states: "Let me win. But if I cannot win, let me be brave in the attempt."

The Olympians train and compete in basketball, volleyball, track and field, gymnastics, roller-skating, canoeing, power lifting, soccer, table tennis, tennis, and others. Age and ability determines the level of competition.

In the United States, the results of local and state games are evaluated to determine the number of Olympians who will compete at the national level. This selection is based on merit, not ability.

The International Special Olympics, with more than one hundred countries participating, is held every two years, with both summer and winter games.

This outstanding program is free to the participants. Because it is not funded by federal money, local Special Olympic organizations look for funding and volunteers in the community.

Call the group in your community that sponsors Special Olympics—often a school or a civic organization—and ask how volunteers from your class can be involved. If you aren't successful there, contact the chapter nearest you. The web site below lists addresses of chapters all around the world.

Special Olympics
1325 G Street NW
Suite 500
Washington, DC 20005
Telephone: 202-628-3630
Fax: 202-824-0200
E-mail: soimail@aol.com
Web site: www.specialolympics.org

CHAPTER 15

Students With
DEVELOPMENTAL
DELAYS

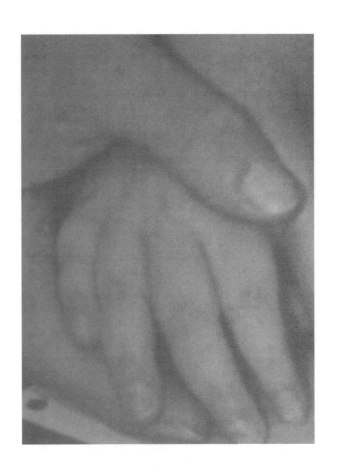

Because of the efforts to include learners with special needs in the regular classroom, the public school system has discovered a lot of children who do not have a diagnosis that would make them eligible for special education services, but who really need some help.

The situation has resulted in an IDEA category of "developmental delay."

IDEA definition

The IDEA definition, in part, states: "Developmental delay refers to children aged three through nine who are experiencing delays, as measured by appropriate diagnostic instruments and procedures, in one or more of the following areas: physical, cognitive, communication, social or emotional, or adaptive development that adversely affect a child's education performance. Other disability categories should be used if they are more descriptive of a young child's strengths and needs." The testing procedures and the collecting of information for determining if the child is eligible is detailed in the law.

An Exceptional Life Story

Angie started attending Sunday school when she was four. Her parents were divorced and she lived with her grandmother. When she came to class, her grandmother's next-door neighbors brought her. Angie always wore clean, attractive clothes. Even though she was quiet compared with the other children, she enjoyed being at Sunday school and did everything the other children did. Her teacher reported to the children's director that she didn't seem to understand everything that was said to her. Her vocabulary was limited. Sometimes she had difficulty getting the correct word. She had difficulty using the playground equipment because of immature motor skills.

As a worker with young children, you may have seen several Angies in your class. You know that the student is not functioning at the level of her age-mates. You know her problem isn't any of the usual disabilities: mental retardation, cerebral palsy, or a learning problem. But she doesn't use language just right. Her fine motor skills are not up to the level of the other children.

Understanding Angie and children like her will be easier if you are aware that she fits into a group of kids often referred to as "at risk." This label means that, because of several factors, children are at risk for developing poor academic skills, and display inappropriate behaviors that will limit their success as students and as adults.

A child can be at risk for one or more of the following reasons:

▼ **Poverty** heads the list. Poverty is often related to learning disabilities, mental retardation, health problems, emotional problems, abuse of children, crime, poor parenting, hunger, poor prenatal care, and substandard housing.

▼ **Homelessness** is another factor. Sadly, it is not just an adult problem. It happens to children. Some 25 percent of the homeless population are chidren. It isn't easy to do homework in a car or a shelter.

▼ **The death of a special person** in the child's life, like a parent or a sibling, can lead to emotional problems, fears, anxiety, learning difficulties, and aggression.

▼ **Living in a single-parent home**, having divorced parents, and losing a sense of belonging can interfere with the typical development processes of the young child.

▼ **Being abused** puts a child at a significant risk. Physical, emotional, sexual abuse, and neglect takes its toll on the child's feelings about himself. It causes development delays, depression, inappropriate habits, and difficulties in relating to people. Abuse happens in all kinds of families.

▼ **Alcohol and drug abuse, teen pregnancy, and juvenile delinquency** complete the sad list of at-risk factors.

If you are teaching a student from an at-risk environment, your emotional input is more important than the educational.

▼ Add positively to the child's self-esteem.
▼ Show a personal interest in the child.
▼ Radiate the feeling, "You matter to me!"
▼ Look for the child's gift.
▼ Convey how much his heavenly Father loves him.

If Angie were in your Sunday school class, what would you do? Two approaches will be helpful. Bombard her with sensory information, and stimulate as many learning channels as possible.

Two exceptional assistants for students with developmental delays are buddies and computers. The buddy helps a child to understand that he is lovable; the computer allows him to play, learn, and express himself without hindrance.

©2001 Jim West

Approach one: bombard with sensory information

From the time a child starts breathing on his own, the sensory system turns on and the learning begins. (Actually, babies learn to recognize their parents' voices before they are born, and mothers often know how their unborn child will react to certain foods she eats!) Through touch, taste, odor, movement, sight, and sound, our brains are filled with the information necessary to relate to our surroundings.

The child with developmental delay has missed opportunities to fill his or her brain. You can stimulate listening, talking, looking, touching, moving, smelling, and tasting through interest centers, music, stories, conversation, pictures and objects, cutting, pasting, finger-painting, games, drama, and much, much more. Integrating the senses doesn't change because a student has a disability. If anything, the disability increases the importance of being sure all of the senses are stimulated when the child is in the classroom. The basic concept is simple: every lesson should include as many activities to stimulate the senses as is practical.

The lesson plan on pages 160 and 161 will serve as an example of the multi-sensory approach.

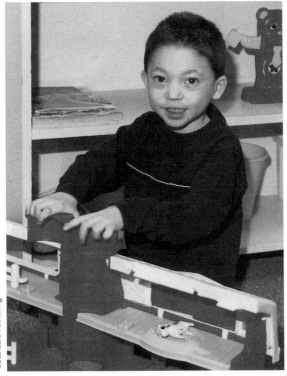

©Standard Publishing

Derik is developmentally delayed, but all the bright colors, interesting people, sights and sounds of Sunday school will stimulate him and help him catch up.

Lesson: Jesus Calms the Storm

Scripture: "One day Jesus and his followers got into a boat. He said to them, 'Come with me across the lake.' And so they started across. While they were sailing, Jesus fell asleep. A big storm blew up on the lake. The boat began to fill with water, and they were in danger.

"The followers went to Jesus and woke him. They said, 'Master! Master! We will drown!'

"Jesus got up and gave a command to the wind and the waves. The wind stopped, and the lake became calm. Jesus said to his followers, 'Where is your faith?'" (Luke 8:22-25, International Children's Bible).

Objectives:
▾ Students will see the sail of the boat and the darkness of night.
▾ Students will hear the sounds of the storm.
▾ Students will feel wind blowing and the movement of waves.
▾ Students will taste the salt water.

Materials:
▾ Tape of thunderstorm
▾ Fans
▾ Air mattress raft
▾ Salt water
▾ Black plastic
▾ Bed sheet or mural paper for sail

Preparation:
▾ Before students come into the room, cover windows with black plastic to darken the room.
▾ Place the air mattress raft in the middle of the room.
▾ Place several fans around the room facing the raft.
▾ Make a salt-water mixture and keep it out of reach of the students.
▾ Plug in tape player.
▾ Using the bed sheet or mural paper, construct a sail on a wall in the classroom.

Title: Jesus Calms the Storm

Procedure:

As students enter the room, ask them to be seated in the raft. Turn off the lights and tell the story. When the story mentions the storm, turn on the tape of the storm and the fans. For added effect, have the classroom aide sprinkle water on the students' faces. After the story is told, turn on one small light and leave the fans and tape running.

Learning Questions:

What do you think it was like on the boat while it was storming and Jesus was sleeping?
If you were one of the followers, would you have asked Jesus to wake up?
What do you think the followers thought when Jesus calmed the storm?
What did Jesus mean by asking, "Where is your faith?"
"We should never forget that God is always in control, even when life is scary and we feel very alone. Do bad things ever happen in your life? Do you sometimes feel like God is a million miles away? Jesus said those are the times we need to have faith. We must believe that God is with us even though we can't see Him."

Ask several students to talk about a time when they were scared. "What did you do?" "What can you do the next time you are frightened?" "Pray, and remember what you learned today: God is always with us."

Closing Prayer:

"Let's ask God to help us when we are scared. Dear God, thank You for loving us and protecting us. We know that even though we can't see You, You are always with us. Please help us in those times when we are scared. Remind us that You are always with us. In Jesus' name, amen."

Approach two: stimulate as many learning channels as possible

It is not always easy to know how any student is learning. Learning occurs by reading and writing, listening, talking, seeing, touching, moving, smelling and tasting. The alert teacher will select those techniques that stimulate the most learning styles.

Some educational techniques and materials are effective learning aids for the child with developmental delays.

▼ Interest centers
▼ Music (cassettes, rhythm band)
▼ Stories
▼ Conversation
▼ Pictures and objects
▼ Videos
▼ Cutting, pasting
▼ Finger paint
▼ Games, clay
▼ Drama, role play

Study this learning-channel wheel and apply it to any technique. Let's consider puppets as an example. Puppets make use of many learning channels: two (listening), three (talking), four (seeing), and six (moving). The other channels could be worked into a puppet activity.

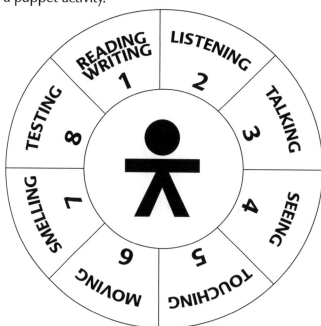

Angie and her little friends may be at risk for learning and behavior problems, but they should not be at risk for learning about the love of Jesus. A good Sunday schoolteacher can prevent that from happening. Knowing Jesus can give their lives meaning and direction.

CHAPTER 16

Students With
TRAUMATIC BRAIN INJURY

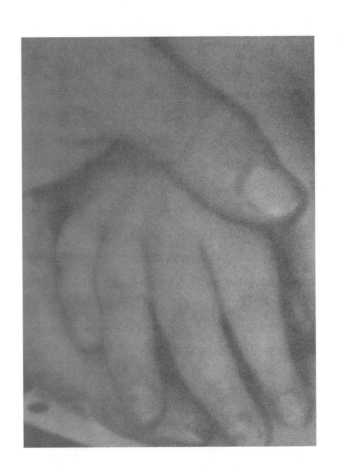

IDEA definition

In 1990, the IDEA made traumatic brain injury a separate special education category and defined it as

"An acquired injury to the brain caused by an external physical force, resulting in total or partial functional disability or psychosocial impairment, or both, that adversely affects a student's educational performance. The term applies to open or closed head injuries resulting in impairments in one or more areas, such as cognition; language; memory; attention; reasoning; abstract thinking; judgment; problem-solving; sensory, perceptual, and motor abilities; psychosocial behavior; physical functions; information processing; and speech. The term does not apply to brain injuries that are congenital or degenerative, or brain injuries induced by birth trauma."

An Exceptional Life Story

Seven-year-old Brad was riding his bike home from the city playground, less than a block from his home. Even though he was safely on the sidewalk, a car left the street and struck his bike. The impact threw the child several feet into the air. His horrified mother, who was watching out the kitchen window, ran to his side. Brad was unconscious and remained so for more than a day. His right arm was broken. The paramedics arrived within minutes and transported him to the local trauma center. The diagnosis was massive brain injury. Surgery was performed to stop the bleeding in the brain.

After a month in the hospital, Brad was transferred to a pediatric rehabilitation center. Emma and Joe, his parents, were pleased that physical, speech, and occupational therapy were successful. Brad was beginning to talk, walk, feed himself, and had even asked to ride his bike.

The parents were concerned about some changes they had noticed. He often complained of being tired and having a headache. They were really bothered by his inability to retrieve the word he needed, his lack of attention, and his apparent loss of cognitive ability. The question they asked Brad's primary doctor is the question of greatest concern for most parents, "What will his future be?"

In many cases of TBI, the answer is that the future will be different. The child will not be the same person he was before. Understanding those changes and helping the child fit into a positive learning environment will help make his future better.

TRAUMATIC BRAIN INJURY

Closed head injury means that the person's brain has been jolted to the point that it moves back and forth, like jelly, and rubs against and/or hits the rough interior of the skull. Often, as in Brad's case, bleeding and swelling occur. The closed injury also puts a lot of pressure on the brain stem, where a lot of information is sent from the brain to the spine and other parts of the body. This area is the center of consciousness and alertness.

Open head injury indicates that a specific area of the brain has been damaged. A gunshot wound is an example. Certain lobes in the brain control various functions. The temporal lobe, for example, is responsible for hearing, language, and speech. An injury to that area of the brain may cause some difficulty in talking, but wouldn't necessarily cause as many personality or emotional problems (controlled by the frontal lobe).

Causes of TBI

The four main causes of traumatic brain injury are
▼ Motor vehicle accidents (more than half of the injuries are related to motorized vehicles)
▼ Falls
▼ Violence
▼ Sport and recreation accidents

Change, change, change

For teachers of students with TBI, the key factor is lots of change.

Changes in cognitive ability:
▼ Attention deficits
▼ Concentration problems
▼ Long/short-term memory
▼ Poor reasoning
▼ Poor judgment
▼ Problems in academics (from an A student to a C student)
▼ Poor processing skills
▼ Weak planning abilities

Changes in speech and language abilities:
▼ Aphasia (can't use language appropriately)
▼ Slow speech
▼ Difficulty selecting a word
▼ Problems following instructions
▼ Immaturity in speech and language usage

▼ Loss of ability to interpret inflection of voice, and body language
▼ While speech may be restored to a useful level, receptive abilities and writing skills will be long-term problems.
▼ Dysarthria, an articulation problem caused by the lack of full use of the tongue

Changes in physical abilities:
▼ Gets tired easily
▼ May start having seizures
▼ Headaches likely
▼ May be changes in gait

Changes in sensory awarness:
▼ Conductive losses (caused by anything that blocks the sound from being processed)
▼ Sensorineural loss (caused by damage to the nerve)
▼ Blurred vision
▼ Changes in visual field

Changes in behavior and emotions:
▼ A new identity is emerging
▼ Self-concept changes
▼ Self-centeredness
▼ Denial of changes in personality
▼ Current reactions will be different from pre-injury ones
▼ Depression is common
▼ Temper outbursts
▼ Anxious
▼ Irritable
▼ Euphoric

©H. Armstrong Roberts

While most physical injuries to the body will heal, a traumatic brain injury will forever change the victim.

▼ Difficulty starting new tasks
▼ Lack of motivation/laziness
▼ Overactivity
▼ Helplessness
▼ Impulsive

Prognosis

A few years ago many people with traumatic brain injuries died. Today more survive. However, there are some facts that have to be dealt with.

▼ The person will cope with change.
▼ Some changes will be temporary; others will be permanent.
▼ The severity of the brain injury is not always an indicator of the long-term effects.

Exceptional Teaching Tips

▼ If you knew the student before the injury, learn to value the person he or she is becoming.
▼ Give simple instructions in concrete terms.
▼ Have the student say the instructions back to you.
▼ Seat the student to achieve his best attention.
▼ Use a lot of visual materials in teaching.
▼ Repeat and review often.
▼ Be quick to let the student know how he is doing.
▼ Give directions both orally and visually.
▼ Extra time might be helpful.
▼ Assign a buddy.
▼ Define words that the person might have forgotten.
▼ Determine on a regular basis if the material is being understood.
▼ Be sure class members understand the needs of their friend with TBI.

Two useful ideas:

Use a tape recorder to record your lesson. The tape will be an excellent review for the child at home. It will also help the parents know what you are accomplishing in the classroom.

Work on developing the self-esteem of the youngster who is struggling with who he was and who he is becoming.

▼ Praise honestly and often.
▼ Provide opportunities for being responsible.
▼ Include the person in other church programs designed for his age-mates.

TRAUMATIC SPINAL CORD INJURY

Sometimes there is confusion about brain and spinal damage. Knowing the basic difference will benefit the teacher's understanding of the student.

The causes of traumatic spinal cord injury (TSCI) are similar to the causes of TBI. The difference in the two categories is that damage to the spine usually results in physical problems only, with few cognitive problems. The severity of the problem is determined by the location on the spine of the damage. From low to high, sections of the spine are called sacral, lumbar, thoracic, and cervical. The higher the damaged area, the more extensive the problems will be. For example, a cervical level damage would be worse than a sacral. If you have a student with TSCI, follow the ideas in the section on physical disabilities. (See pages 105 through 116.)

SHAKEN BABY SYNDROME

I really don't like providing this information, but it is necessary. When we asked churches to give diagnoses of the children they were working with, SBS appeared on the lists.

SBS occurs when the arms, legs, chest, or shoulders are used to shake an infant or young child. It is the leading cause of head injury in infants. The shaking can cause bleeding in the brain and around the eyes. Because the child's head is so large and the neck muscles are so weak, the injury occurs. The results of SBS damage can be

▼ Vision problems, even blindness
▼ Death
▼ Developmental disabilities
▼ Mental retardation
▼ Seizures
▼ Learning problems
▼ Paralysis
▼ Speech and language problems
▼ Hearing loss
▼ Cerebral palsy
▼ Behavior problems

When the baby is taken to the hospital, the examination reveals a closed head injury, unconsciousness, bleeding in the retina, blood in the brain, large head size.

Some Terrible Facts

▼ Fifty thousand cases occur annually in the United States.

▼ Head trauma is the most common cause of irreversible damage and death in infants.

▼ One out of four dies.

▼ Fathers, and mother's boyfriend, are typical shakers.

▼ Female shakers tend to be baby-sitters and caregivers other than mothers.

▼ Excessive crying, toilet-training problems, and jealousy lead to the most severe shaking.

▼ Not many of the children recover completely.

Special Ministry Suggestions

▼ Older couples in the congregation should keep an eye on the heavy schedules of young couples with young children and offer to baby-sit.

▼ Teenagers should be told about how to prevent damage to babies.

▼ Have an elective class taught by older members of the church for younger couples. Stress the importance of controlling anger in dealing with children. Share ideas that have worked for you. I heard a great one. The mother would vacuum after she changed her daughter who would continue to cry. The noise drowned out the crying!

▼ Provide programs that provide occasional respite.

CHAPTER 17

PROVIDING CHRISTIAN EDUCATION
for Students With Disabilities

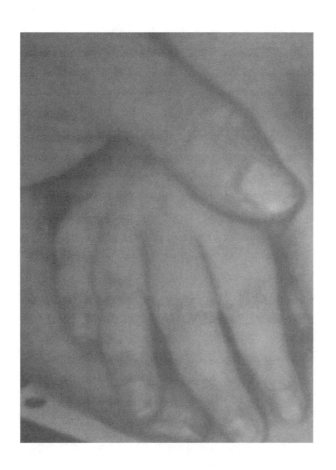

When a congregation is ready to start an inclusive ministry, the process is easy. Twelve steps will lead to the goal of making the gospel of Jesus available to students of all abilities.

STEP ONE: Determine the approach that your congregation will follow.

STEP TWO: Involve the entire congregation and the leadership.

STEP THREE: Inform the congregation and the community of your plan.

STEP FOUR: Train the staff.

STEP FIVE: Organize a welcoming classroom.

STEP SIX: Adapt curricula and select good methods for teaching.

STEP SEVEN: Prepare the students for the inclusion experience.

STEP EIGHT: Learn about the student to be included.

STEP NINE: Interview the family.

STEP TEN: Prepare the Individual Christian Education Plan.

STEP ELEVEN: Anticipate the person's future in the congregation.

STEP TWELVE: Enjoy knowing that you are making an eternal difference in the life of the person with a disability and his family.

STEP ONE:
Determine an Approach

Take a survey of your congregation to locate persons and families who are dealing with disability. In most cases you will be surprised at the numbers. Congregations who report, "We don't have any people with disabilities or we would start something for them," discover when they look that they have several. Start with a simple insert in the bulletin or church paper. The survey on the next page is a sample. Adapt it to your situation.

©Standard Publishing

Whether you mainstream children with disabilities or create a separate class for them, the teacher-to-student ratio is high. In this class, because the bigger boy with his back to the camera is an assistant, you can see that the ratio is almost one-to-one.

DISABILITY SURVEY

This congregation wants to minister to people of all abilities. People who have mental retardation, autism, learning disabilities, hearing loss, blindness, and emotional problems, among other disabilities, need to know the saving grace of Jesus, and deserve to know His love. We want to learn how we can better serve persons with disabilities of all ages, as well as their families. Please help us by completing the following questionnaire and return it to the church office.

Do you or a member of your family have a disability?

YES   NO

Do you have a friend or neighbor who has a disability?

YES   NO

What is the nature of your friend's or family member's disability?

Hearing impairment	Learning Disability
Autism	Mental illness
Mental Retardation	Cerebral palsy
Stroke	Visual impairment
Down syndrome	Traumatic brain injury
Other (please explain)_____	

_____

What age is your friend? _____

Does your friend or relative attend church regularly?

YES   NO

If not, would he/she like to?

YES   NO

What can we do to help include your friend or relative in the fellowship of our church?

Provide transportation
Provide a specialized Sunday school class
Provide better accessibility
Other (please explain)

_____
_____

Does your friend or relative have needs related to the following?

Counseling	Assistance with weekly shopping
Respite car	Transportation for appointments
Amplification	Sign language interpretation
Support group	Braille Bible study materials
Large-print Bible	Medical equipment (specify)

_____

Other (please explain)_____
_____
_____

How can we best provide support and encouragement for your friend or relative?

_____
_____

As a member of this congregation, can you help?

YES   NO

I am interested in learning more about this ministry.

YES   NO

I would like to be trained as a volunteer in the following: (Please circle all areas that interest you.)

Education
Sunday schoolteacher
Sunday school assistant
Biweekly Bible study leader at residential facilities

Respite Care Programs
Mother's Day Out (monthly)
Friday Night Live (bimonthly)
Saturday Morning Break (monthly)

Transportation
Driver (Sunday mornings)
Driver (weekly activities)

Prayer Partners

Inclusion Assistant

Name_____

Address_____

City/State/Zip_____

_____

Phone_____

I am	under 18	19-40	41-60	over 60

E-mail_____

Study the results

Appoint a disability ministry team to study the results of your survey. The following statements will help guide your team:

▼ When a parent or guardian with a child with a disability comes to our church, we will include the child in the class for his age group.

▼ We will provide the family members with a support system that will allow them to become active in the church and to pursue their own spiritual development.

▼ We will provide the student with an assistant until he is able to manage the schedule on his own.

▼ If the student is too severely disabled for a regular class, we will provide a learning setting that will permit him to be with his age-mates some of the time.

▼ We will determine the student's mental age in order to assess his ability or readiness to embrace faith.

▼ Cerebral palsy, autism, fragile X syndrome, a hearing loss, or any other physical or emotional disability should not be a barrier to developing the student's spiritual being.

▼ Every person, regardless of ability, needs to know that Jesus loves him.

▼ We will pray that God will help us understand all of our students. We will ask Him for patience, warmth, openness, and caring.

Write a mission statement, using the following as an example:

This ministry is dedicated to serving children, youth, and adults with disabilities and their families. We believe that individuals with disabilities are precious gifts from God and are here specifically to teach us lessons that we might never learn by ourselves. We consider it a privilege and a direct call from God to reach out to those who are disabled because this ministry represents the very heart of God. We are committed, not just to serving these individuals, but to empowering them to become vital members of the body of Christ.

Write your own mission statement below:

_____
_____
_____
_____
_____
_____
_____
_____
_____
_____
_____
_____
_____

STEP TWO:
Involve the Congregation and Leadership

▼ The leadership sees every person, regardless of ability, as valuable and worthy of God's love.
▼ The senior minister is involved and supports the effort.
▼ The congregation will be aware of the needs, especially the spiritual needs, of students with disabilities.
▼ We will host a disability awareness Sunday or weekend. Such an event will enable members to
  – know more about people with disabilities
  – be more sensitive to their needs
  – know that their spiritual needs are as important as those of typical people
  – be motivated to include them
  – know that the most important part of the person is his soul

An outline for a Disability Awareness Sunday:
▼ **Theme** examples: "The Variety in Ability." "Christ's Love Is Inclusive and Accessible."
▼ **Sermon.** Using Scripture that describes Jesus' encounter with a person with a disability is always good. It gives a biblical foundation for the outreach.
▼ **Music.** Using any of the many hymns written by Fanny Crosby will speak to the value of people with disabilities using their talents in the church. (Fanny Crosby was blind from the age of six weeks.)
▼ **Special music.** There are many possibilities, but a good one is, "Sometimes Miracles Hide" (Word, 1991).
▼ **Testimony.** Having a family tell of the importance of developing faith in their child helps the congregation see that all Christian parents treasure faith and want their children to have it.
▼ **Personnel with disabilities.** Use people with disabilities to serve as ushers, sing, play an instrument, read Scripture.
▼ **Bulletin cover.** Use a bulletin cover that stresses the theme and purpose of the day.
▼ **Sunday school.** Have every teacher in the department teach the same lesson. A story from Jesus' ministry can be applied to all age groups.
▼ **Follow up.** Your disability awareness weekend will generate many good inten-

Two young men with cerebral palsy enjoy the freedom of movement and of expression that a computer provides for them.

©Jeff Greenberg/Photi, Inc.

tions. Capture them. Use a survey to identify needs in the church family and the members who are willing to be involved in meeting those needs.

▼ **Ideas.** Have one member of the congregation spend the morning in a wheelchair, another blindfolded, another with both hands bandaged, and another wearing earplugs. At some point in the day, have them report their experiences to help everyone get some indication of how disability feels.

Note: Disability awareness information can be distributed through inserts in church publications, projected on a screen before the service, or left on display at the welcome center. The method that suits your congregation should be used.

STEP THREE:
Inform the Community and Visitors

▼ When the community learns of your effort, word of mouth will become your best advertisement.

▼ Share the information with parent groups in the community.

▼ Ask the local newspaper to do an article on your program.

▼ Prepare a sheet describing the program, including who-to-get-in-touch-with information, and distribute it to program facilitators in the community who work with children with special needs. Note: Because of confidentiality laws, these organizations cannot give you names, but they can send the sheets home with the students.

▼ Use ads in the Yellow Pages to say that your congregation welcomes people with disabilities.

▼ Provide information at the welcome center about the nature and locations of programs for persons with disabilities.

▼ Develop an attractive brochure that describes your disability ministry. Be creative.

STEP FOUR:
Train the Staff

The most important people on the team are the teachers who will be responsible for guiding the spiritual development of students with and without disabilities in their classrooms.

The qualifications of an inclusive teacher

▼ Cares about students of all abilities.

▼ Believes that what she is teaching is important and will make an eternal difference.

▼ Does not have to have high-achieving students in order to feel successful.

▼ Doesn't mind doing a little extra for a student who needs it.

▼ Is willing to learn about a student's disability.

▼ Enjoys training people to assist in the teaching process.

▼ Is able to make quick decisions under pressure.

The Christian education department of the church should provide the teachers with the assurance of prayer, a library of materials, quick access to information on disabilities, and plenty of assistance.

Peggy Willocks, a fifteen-year veteran in the classroom and a person with a disability herself, presents some questions that each teacher should answer with a resounding YES!

▼ First and foremost, have I prayed about this student's situation and my influence on his or her spiritual life?
▼ Am I properly informed as to this child's condition, and am I sure that the measures taken are appropriate?
▼ Do I truly believe in and encourage the success of this child in my classroom?
▼ Am I encouraging the acceptance of this child by the other students through my example?
▼ Do I explain questions by the other students in a tactful, loving way?
▼ Am I treating this child fairly, avoiding singling out the child, and fostering his or her independence?
▼ Is the environment or room arrangement such that the student is able to move freely and safely about the room?
▼ Is placement of the student in relationship to the teacher adequate for the child to see and/or hear well, or where I can monitor possible situations quickly?
▼ Have prior arrangements or modifications been made so that the child can interact with both students and teacher in an independent manner?

Three other groups who need training:
▼ Assistants
▼ Buddies, children in the class who will assist the child and make him feel welcome
▼ Peer tutors, older children who will help with a lesson if a child needs to have some extra attention

Where do you recruit volunteers for your program?
▼ Anyone who is not already overcommitted
▼ Senior members who have so much to share
▼ Singles
▼ Members of youth groups
▼ College students
▼ Families who will minister as a team
▼ Older elementary-age children to be buddies or peer tutors

What do they need to know?
▼ An overview of disability
▼ Specific information about the disability of the child they will be assisting
▼ A specific job description that states what the task is and how long the volunteer will do it

▼ Some basic etiquette
▼ Emphasis of the purpose of the assignment: Sharing Jesus' love to make an eternal difference in the life of a child with a disability

How should volunteers be treated?

▼ Give adequate supervision. No one wants to feel all alone.
▼ Meet together as a group on a monthly basis to evaluate, plan, and prepare.
▼ Provide continuous opportunities for training and education by sharing articles, videos, and other materials that will educate about specific disabilities, and reports on cutting edge information. Pay fees for volunteers to attend seminars and workshops.
▼ Explore networking possibilities where individuals and groups engaged in disability ministry meet together to share ideas and resources.
▼ If an individual incurs expenses while volunteering, reimburse him in a timely fashion.
▼ On a regular basis, send notes and postcards after each event to thank every volunteer who participated.
▼ Plan an annual appreciation luncheon or banquet.

Where do I go for training material?

This book can be used in a variety of ways to train volunteers to work in the inclusion process for students with disabilities. Use the suggestions offered here to arrange training sessions specific to your needs.

A three-session training program

Session One: The Students We Include

During this session participants will be introduced to the range of disabilities people have, study their basic characteristics, and learn the best approaches for including them in a typical class.

▼ Display the list of people with disabilities via PowerPoint, on a transparency, or by some other method.
▼ Discuss the definition for each category.
▼ List the three or four most notable characteristics of each group.
▼ Point out suggestions for making inclusion easier for the child.
▼ Talk about any adaptations or changes in the classroom.

Session Two: The Steps We Follow for Their Inclusion

This session will provide the group with the philosophy of the program, the methods for carrying it out, and the responsibility for nurturing the student spiritually.

▼ Before the session make copies of any forms, evaluations, etc., that the trainees need to have for understanding how the program works.
▼ Have a discussion of each of the twelve steps for "Including a Child in the Christian Education Program."
▼ Explain how the forms are to be completed.
▼ Allow plenty of time for questions and answers.

***Session Three:* The Way We Support Families**

Purpose: This section of the study will outline the approaches to ministering *with*, not *to*, the family of the child with a disability.

▼ We will assist the family in meeting their general needs.
▼ We will learn the right words to say to them.
▼ We will assist with respite care.
▼ We will be attentive to the other children in the family.
▼ We will serve as advocates in the student's education program.

Training assistants, peer tutors, and buddies

This session is designed to provide information about a specific student to be included in the class. The participants will be those people who will assist the teacher.

▼ Review the section of the book that discusses the disability, i.e., autism.
▼ Look over the information the parents provided during their interview and the results of the religious matters examination (see pages 192 and 199).
▼ Discuss specific approaches that need to be taken with the student.
▼ This session could be accomplished in ninety minutes.

Other training possibilities are sessions for training members of the congregation as advocates in special education, and training of respite-care workers.

STEP FIVE:
Organize a Welcoming Classroom

Since you will be using a regular classroom, the following items will help you determine if it is suited to the needs of students with disabilities. The following suggestions will help you create a positive learning environment.

This child would be able to join her classmates in completing the puzzle if the table was kidney-shaped to accommodate her wheelchair.

©H. Armstrong Roberts

▼ The classroom should be attractive and clean.
▼ It should be uncluttered.
▼ It should have space to store materials to keep them out of the sight of hyper-active eyes.
▼ It should be roomy. A student in a wheelchair or one who uses a cane needs extra space.
▼ It should bright. Use as much natural light as possible.
▼ It should be well ventilated.
▼ It should have a rest room or be close to one.
▼ It should be as noise free as possible.
▼ It should be safe and accessible for students of all abilities.
▼ It should have a space for a student to be alone.

Again, Peggy Willocks makes a great statement about the classroom setting.

"The arrangement of the classroom is of vital importance not only to the student in a wheelchair or one with physical limitations (crutches, braces, artificial or missing limbs, etc.) but also to those with emotional/behavioral disturbances or mental deficiencies.

"The room should be arranged to provide free-flowing traffic and safe movement for students with physical and visual problems. This can be accomplished with wide-open areas, wide doorways, tables and chairs at the proper heights, and flat or smooth flooring surfaces. Modified furniture may need to be purchased (for example, a kidney-shaped table for a student in a wheelchair).

"Room arrangement is also important for the proper instruction of students with visual and hearing problems. The student with special needs should be located near the areas used by the teacher for instruction. The physical location of the student with emotional or behavioral difficulties would likewise be of paramount importance to allow the teacher a rapid response to a situation that may threaten the safety of the child with a disability and the other children. For the child with a learning disability, arrange the room so that minimal distractions from simultaneous activities will occur. Blocking devices for visual or sound stimuli such as dividers or walls can be utilized. Avoid too many mobile stimuli for this student, such as decorations suspended from the ceiling."

STEP SIX:
Adapting Materials and Selecting Methods

Good Sunday schoolteachers often ask, "Where do I get materials for working with kids who have disabilities?" The question has several answers.

If the student is being included in the class with his peers, then the answer is, adapt the materials you are already using.

For the student who is blind, find a person in your community who is willing to put part of the lesson sheets into braille for your student.

For the student who is visually impaired, enlarge the lesson on the copy machine, provide a magnifying glass, or do whatever is necessary to make the print larger.

For the student who has a learning disability, color code the parts of the lesson you want to stress. You can do it with a highlighter or use a transparency designed with colors to stress the main points of the lesson.

If you want to ask a student with a learning disability to read, call him during the week and ask his family to practice with him.

For the student who is hard-of-hearing, put the important parts of the lesson on PowerPoint (or other means) and project it. This will help the student and his classmates as well. Putting the lesson on overheads will serve the same purpose. Projecting the instructions for the class will also help the student who is hard-of-hearing. The more visual the lesson is, the better it will be for the student who has auditory problems.

For the student who is deaf, the lesson materials will be fine. He can read them. Like the student who is hard-of-hearing, the more visual you can make the lesson the better. The best assurance you can provide that the student is learning is to have an interpreter available.

For the student who has mental retardation, the materials will likely be a bit over his head. But provide him the same materials you do for the other members. Give him a workbook! He is part of the class and having his own workbook will help make him feel that way. The pictures will be age-appropriate. When there are table activities, simplify an activity or two and have a peer tutor help the student with it. Don't call on him to read unless you know that he can read and you have asked in advance. Ask him to do the motor-type activities.

For the student whose disability is severe, think about preparing activities for him to take home. He can use these for his devotional thoughts and as a reminder of the lesson. If the lesson is about God's creativity, make a scrapbook of items God made. The sky is the limit. Use cotton for clouds. Glue some beans to a page. Pour some perfume on the page. Instruct the family how to assist the child with the take-home activity you have prepared.

Watching the student work and seeing how he reacts to materials will provide you with more ideas on how to adapt the lesson materials to maximize his potential.

Selecting Curriculum

If you have the opportunity to select the curriculum, be sure it meets the following criteria:

▼ The purposes of the lessons are stated clearly.
▼ There are lots of suggestions for the ways of applying the lessons.
▼ The teaching methods stress use of all the senses.
▼ Not all the activities are paper and pencil activities.
▼ The language is clear.
▼ The pictures and illustrations are age-appropriate.

There are some specially prepared materials available, however they are not easy to find. They are most often prepared for adults, are often for only one quarter of study, and they go out of print quickly. In the resource section, we recommend *Dimensions of Faith and Congregational Ministries With Persons With Developmental Disabilities and Their Families*. A quick review of the section, "Religious Education Guides and Curricula," reveals all of the criteria listed above.

There are three curricula that I find useful:

▼ **Scripture Bites** is a Bible-based curriculum for preschoolers that offers a wide variety of multi-sensory activities. The short themes can easily be adapted for teaching students with disabilities. It is available from Standard Publishing, 800-543-1353.

▼ **Friendship Series** is a three-year curriculum for youth and adults. It includes a group leader's kit, teacher's manual, and student resources. (Amistad is the Spanish version.) For prices and other information contact CRC Publications, 2850 Kalamazoo Avenue SE, Grand Rapids, MI 49560, or call 616-246-0842.

▼ **Breakthrough** provides lessons, resources, and information for sharing the gospel with people with mental retardation. This is the one I use the most. It gives the idea for a lesson, gives the scriptural basis, and offers activity suggestions. With that information, I can make the ideas meet my students' needs, teach my faith group's theological positions, and add whatever details are the most helpful. It is available from Bethesda Lutheran Homes and Services, 700 Hoffman Drive, Watertown, WI 53094-6294.

Whatever the material or the method, it is important to stress to your students that the lessons you are teaching are from God's Word. In my own Sunday school classroom, I have a large cutout of the Bible complete with a red marker. This cutout, or frame, attaches to a whiteboard. Each Sunday, I write on the board, outside the Bible, the name of the lesson. Inside the Bible I write the reference and a very short summary of the lesson. Anytime a student gets distracted, or forgets what he is supposed to be learning, he needs only to look at the board to bring him back into focus.

Technology assists

The student with a disability in your classroom will likely have been exposed to some form of technology, either in his education program, his therapy, or his home. His favorite toy might have a computer component! It is a good idea to be familiar with the electronic world that touches your student's world. As the teacher, you need to know about any device he uses to give him more independence, such as his communication device, or the adapted switch (breath-controlled, finger-controlled) he uses to control his wheelchair or computer, or any other device. Ask the family to give you a demonstration of the equipment.

It is also a good idea to use the computer as a teaching tool. If you don't feel comfortable with this idea, find someone in your congregation who is computer savvy. Ask that person to assist you in developing a meaningful use of the computer in your classroom. Doing what you can to augment lessons will enhance the multi-sensory approach to teaching that is so important to good learning.

Further, it is a good idea to find sources for computer software that might assist you with teaching. The market for general and special education is full of possibilities, and there are a growing number of Bible-related resources. The teaching CDs from Focus on the Family or Compton's Multimedia Biblical Encyclopedia are good examples. If your church has the equipment necessary to take advantage of this material, you will find it most helpful. Check with a Christian bookstore or surf the net. Call other Christian educators and ask if they have found good software.

Finally, it is a good idea to explore the possibilities for using cyberspace to find ideas to help you teach your students with special needs about Jesus' love.
▼ Since most people are familiar with the Internet, encourage them to use search engines to locate interesting facts to illustrate a lesson. Or, they can find lesson material from a number of good Christian sites.
▼ Think about developing a web site or organizing an Internet community where you display your students' work. This is an excellent way to include the student with the disability right along with his classmates. Use this site to keep the parents of your students informed about how their children are doing in your class.
▼ Since children with disabilities are often sick, consider using e-mail to send the lesson so that it can be taught at home.
▼ When you are teaching a lesson on missions, arrange to send and receive e-mail from the classroom to a missionary supported by your congregation.
▼ For the student who communicates more effectively with the computer, get permission from the publisher to scan the lesson material.
▼ Expose your students to Christian web sites. Prepare a list of sites you think would be beneficial. Include devotional sites such as www.standardpub.com; www.backtothebible.org/devotions; www.gospel.com/rbc/utmost.
▼ Review and include secular sites aimed at helping people with disabilities. Some good ones are www.icanonline.net; www.newmobility.com; www.ebility.com.

Four Favorite Methods of Teaching

Storytelling

Through the years, many teachers have responded to the request, "Tell me a story." The result has been many lessons learned, behaviors altered, and hearts delighted. Storytelling is a good teaching tool to use in teaching students of all abilities. The following notes will help the teacher maximize the use of storytelling.

Why use storytelling?

▼ It builds imaginative skills.
▼ It helps increase short attention spans.
▼ It gives life to important ideas.
▼ It adds pleasure to learning.

How can the story be most effective?

▼ Select a single purpose.
  - The story should be brief.
  - Omit complicated details that don't fit the purpose.
▼ Know the details.
  - Don't read it, tell it!
▼ Define the story by considering this list:
  - How will the story begin?
  - How will it end?
  - How will I make the individual characters stand out?
▼ Use delivery techniques to heighten the interest level.
  - Vary your voice.
  - Exaggerate for emphasis.
  - Move at appropriate times in the narration.
  - Employ conversation between characters in the story.
▼ Gear the story toward the student with disabilities.
  - Even though your student may act younger than his chronological age, the emphasis of the story should be age-appropriate. In a series of suggestions for applying the story, include items that the student with disabilities can do.
  - If the story uses a custom or practice that the student would not know, omit or change it.
▼ Use voice and language that will enhance the quality of your speech.
  - This is essential to the success of storytelling for students with developmental delays.
  - Don't talk down to the listeners. The best approach is to talk up to them.
  - Select words that are within the student's vocabulary level.
  - Speak slowly.
  - Use good English.
▼ Augment the story.
  - Use a puppet.
  - Use pictures to accent the main points.
  - Let the students act out the story.
  - Any addition to the story that uses the senses will help it.
  - Apply the story to the student's life.

Jesus, the master Teacher, used the story as part of His teaching methods. His stories, applied to the lives of the student with disabilities, will serve as excellent lesson materials. Old Testament stories will enhance the special learning session as well. Contemporary stories, properly applied, serve to delight the class. All learners can benefit from a properly applied story. As the teacher becomes proficient at using the method, the learner will often request, "Tell me a story."

Music

Music is a universal teaching tool. It works. I still hum the tune that taught me the books of the Bible. Students with any disability will benefit from music, even if it is no more than listening. Consider the following:

▼ Learn memory verses or books of the Bible by setting them to music.
▼ Learn a Scripture passage by singing it to an already familiar tune.
▼ Learn to "sign" a song in American Sign Language. This approach will give the student with a hearing impairment a chance to be the teacher.
▼ Make a rebus song chart to help students learn a new song. It is a great idea for students with learning problems.
▼ Choose songs that teach and reinforce Christian behaviors and social skills.
▼ Play games with music that strengthen listening skills.
▼ Learn songs that foster the development of self-esteem. Great for kids with emotional problems.
▼ Use music along with exercise.

- Teach children to play instruments in a rhythm band. (I remember a little guy with severe physical problems who used a head wand to ring a bell tied to his wheelchair. I also remember that his peers without disabilities disrupted the Sunday morning performance in the auditorium because for the first time he did it right!)
- Sing just for the fun and pleasure it brings.

Drama

For the student with a disability in your class, drama will be a good learning tool. It is easy to assume that the student with mental retardation or a physical disability will not enjoy this activity. However, the most enthusiastic wise man I have ever seen was a boy with autism who had to have a nonspeaking part. Since that time, his teachers tell me that he often signs (his method of communication) that he is ready to be a wise man again.

Include students with disabilities in dramas done by the children's department. Use lots of **role play**. It is a good way to get students who have language problems to express themselves. **Skits** offer a fun way to understand the details of the Bible story. **Finger plays** encourage fine motor skills while reinforcing a lesson. Making a class **video** reveals creativity, and gives the student with a disability tangible proof that he is a welcome, active member of his class.

Interest Centers

Interest centers in the classroom provide learning opportunities for students because they can touch and interact. An interest center is an excellent way to have an experience available for the student with a disability who needs to be away from the group for a while because of inappropriate behavior or who could profit from a one-on-one learning time with a peer tutor. Select centers that help the students develop or express their feelings. You will learn the needs of the student who has a disability. Develop a center that fills that need.

An Odor Center

In baby food jars, put several smelly things. Blindfold the student and have him guess, by the odor, what the thing is when you open the jar.

A Touch Center

Select objects that are rough, smooth, square, round, warm, cold, etc. Let the student look at all of them. Ask him to close his eyes while you select an object to go into a sack. Tell him to feel the object in the sack (without looking!) and tell you what it is.

A "How Am I Feeling?" Center

Paste pictures of people whose faces show a wide range of emotion. Ask the student to tell you what the person is feeling. Ask him which pictures shows how he is feeling. Talk to him about how he is feeling.

Technology opens a new world where a person is not judged by appearance, and communication is quick (or at least, quicker). For example, I received an e-mail from a young man with a disability seeking information about attending college. He outlined his goals for his life and his plan for accomplishing them. His use of language was impressive. While I knew there was a disability, I was a bit surprised when he informed me that he could not speak, walk, or take care of all his personal needs. Beneath the disability is a wonderful human being who wants to be accepted, loved, and productive. Technology can be a factor in helping him achieve these "everyone wants those" goals.

STEP SEVEN:
Prepare the Students for the Inclusion Experience

When a student with a disability attends your class, prepare the members without disabilities for the experience. The overall goal is to make everyone feel comfortable. If the student with the disability can be open and honest about his or her situation, the goal has been achieved. If the members of the group are accepting, the goal has been achieved.

An Exceptional Life Story

Talking to children in Vacation Bible Schools has provided me with a lot of good opportunities to teach children about disability. On the first day of a VBS session I talked to fifty five-year-olds about what it means to be disabled, making the point that the most important part of us is inside, not outside. When the session was over, an enthusiastic young man who had another member of the group in tow encountered me.

He announced, "Nathan is handicappeded."

I asked Nathan what his disability was.

"Spina bifida," was the quick, almost proud, reply.

Deciding that I wanted to use Nathan in the next day's lesson, I called his mother for permission. She gladly approved, reporting, "When I asked Nathan what he learned in Vacation Bible School today, he answered, 'It is OK to have spina bifida.'"

Use a four-part preparation program:
▼ Deal directly with the students' reaction to disability with positive responses.
▼ Enhance positive attitudes with positive experiences.
▼ Anchor the lessons in Jesus' teachings.
▼ Develop a reading program.

Deal with the students' reaction to disability with positive comments. See page 188 for ideas of how to respond.

Enhance positive attitudes with positive experiences.
▼ Help children use appropriate language. Stress the person's name and not his diagnosis. Explain "people-first" language. For example, "Jessica has cerebral palsy." (See page fifty-one for other ideas.)
▼ Don't suggest that "We are all disabled in some way." Such statements are meant to help the persons with disabilities feel equal, but that is not what the child sees. He can run; his friend with a brace can't. Avoid stressing that persons with disabilities are special. All of us are special in God's sight.
▼ Expose children to warm, open adults with disabilities. I know a lady who uses her wheelchair as a classroom. When she notices a child having trouble with her presence, she starts a conversation, offers a free ride, and lets the child touch her leg brace. Touching teaches youngsters that a person with a disability is a person. Ask adults with disabilities if they will come into the classroom and allow the children to touch them and ask questions.
▼ Remind parents that their children will pick up their attitudes even though they are never spoken. Children will copy what they see and hear, or think they see and hear.
▼ Give children examples of the benefits they will receive from associating with

Prepare Students for the Inclusion Experience

Reaction: Children see disabling conditions as disease. They fear they will catch what their friend has. Mother has warned, "Don't you sit with him; you will catch his cold." Disabilities are seen as health problems to them.

Response: Assure your class that a disability cannot be caught. If a child is concerned about playing with a child with Down syndrome, explain what the condition is. Say: "You have 46 chromosomes. Twenty-three came from your mom and 23 came from your dad. For some reason, your friend has 47. What he has is called Down syndrome. Since your body already has all the chromosomes it needs, you can't get Down syndrome by playing with him."

Reaction: When children look at people with disabilities, they are using an important avenue of learning: vision. Mother, probably, has told them not to stare, so they think it is bad to look. But looking is helping them learn.

Response: Because children look to learn, teach the difference between a friendly look and a stare. After you model the right way to look, let the children practice. Then give an example. Use cerebral palsy. All cerebral palsy is caused by brain damage. Explain that when a person has cerebral palsy, we can tell which side of the brain is damaged by looking. If the right arm and leg do not work well, it means the left side of the brain is hurt. A direct, brief answer will take care of the questions.

Reaction: Children naturally mimic the characteristics they see in people. They are exploring how it would feel if they themselves were disabled.

Response: Explain to the child that the wrong of imitating his friend is that it will hurt his friend's feelings. Suggest that he demonstrate how his new friend walks for his family later, or that he can experiment with the limp to see how it feels in his bedroom with the door closed. It doesn't take long for the feeling of his friend's condition to get in the child's system. It is not likely to occur again!

their friends who have disabilities. One of my special friends is a young lady with Down syndrome. She has faced not being able to drive, knowing she's not like everyone else, and lots of other realities that would sadden most people; however, she is one of the most positive people I know. Her notes affirming our friendship and her occasional visits enrich my life. No matter how long it has been since we have seen each other, she reminds me that she has missed me.

▼ Encourage children to do something for people with disabilities. A note, a card, a small gift, or a visit are all good ways of expressing concern. Such actions can lead to more involvement in the lives of persons with disabilities.

▼ Encourage children without disabilities to be peer tutors and buddies in programs that include children with disabilities. This approach builds good attitudes, trains future leaders, and presents people as people.

Anchor the lessons in Jesus' teachings.

Children will be delighted when encouraged to take the roof off for their friends with disabilities. When four of his friends took a man with a physical disability to Jesus (Mark 2:1-12), the crowd surrounding Him was so big they couldn't get in. So, they carried him to the roof, made a hole, and lowered the man to the healing presence of Jesus. Jesus said that the faith of his friends caused the healing. Children will also be impressed by the fact that Jesus touched people with disabilities.

Develop a reading program.

Because children enjoy reading or being read to, plan a project that will lead children to a broader understanding of the disability community. The market has many excellent children's books on a variety of disabilities—learning disabilities, spina bifida, hearing losses, Down syndrome, and many others. Readers can read the materials themselves. Nonreaders can have a reading circle. But in either case provide discussion topics, good answers to questions, and exposure to people with disabilities.

Special Alert!

If the student to be included has a serious behavior problem, be extra careful in preparing the members of the class. Some preliminary planning is necessary.

▼ Meet with the parents to discuss the behavior. (Refer to the parent/ guardian interview on page 199.)

▼ Ask about the nature of the behavior. Does he hit? Bite? Throw objects? Run?

▼ Is he on medication for his behavior?

▼ Does he have a behavior modification plan?

▼ Does he receive other professional help?

▼ Is the behavior improving?

Some work with the class is useful.

▼ Openly discuss the student with the entire class and staff.

▼ Explain that his problem causes the behavior and he can't help it.

▼ Clarify that their friend's misbehavior doesn't give them the right to do the same.

▼ Give the children some ownership of the problem. (During a visit to a class-room to observe the behavior of a young boy, he had a tantrum. The teacher quickly brought the behavior under control. A cute little girl sitting by me offered this explanation, "He is like that. He can't help it. Sometimes I touch him and tell him it will be OK.")

▼ Stay in touch with the family about success and failures.

▼ Be patient.

▼ Pray that the God of peace will improve the student's behavior.

Reverse the process

Just as the students without disabilities need some assistance in adjusting to the situation, so will the student with disabilities.

▼ Prior to the first class, visit the classroom with the child, his parents, and a cou-ple of members of the class.

▼ Explain the routine.

▼ Show the child where he will sit.

▼ Ask him if he has any fears about the new situation. If so, answer openly.

▼ Request that the family bring him early on his first day.

An idea with merit

Consider holding an intergenerational class in order to include the student with a disability in a wider circle of the congregation. Occasionally, arrange for a group of older and younger adults, teenagers, children, and the students with disabili-ties to meet together for a lesson. Select an appropriate theme, such as "How to relate to people who have disabilities." Teach a Scripture-based lesson and follow it with a lot of activities that will encourage relationships within the group. Games should be aimed at the purpose of the session.

This intergenerational approach has a lot of good benefits. It permits those who might not otherwise have the opportunity to meet this person, to meet him. It gives the person with the disability a sense of a caring community. It can lead teens and adults to volunteer for the congregation's disability program.

This is an idea with merit. Try it!

STEP EIGHT:
Learn About the Student

Who is he? What does he know about religious matters? Learning this information can be accomplished with the forms on the following pages. Use these forms as samples and make your own, adding items that will help you understand the person's abilities.

STUDENT INFORMATION

Name_____ Age_____ Birthday___/___/___

Hobbies_____

Favorite pastime _____

Favorite friend _____

Favorite food _____

What does he do best? _____

What are his strengths? _____

_____

What tasks can he handle alone? _____

What does he do poorest? _____

What are his weaknesses? _____

_____

With what tasks does he need help? _____

_____

How does he spend his leisure time? _____

_____

How does his disability limit his functioning?_____

_____

EVALUATING KNOWLEDGE OF RELIGIOUS CONCEPTS

Basic Information

Name_____ Age_____ Birthday__/__/__

Address_____

_____

Telephone_____ E-mail _____Grade level in school_____

Parents' names_____

Siblings' names_____

_____

Does the family attend church regularly? _____

What is the family history with church? _____

What does he know about religious matters?

In order to help the person, you also need to know what he knows about the Bible, Jesus, God, and other religious concepts. This following survey will help you.

SECTION ONE:
General Information

Materials: Bible and five pictures:
1 Jesus with children (including a child with a disability)
2 The devil (red man, horns, pointed tail, etc.)
3 A happy face and a sad face
4 Boys fighting
5 Boys shaking hands

Question/Task	Desired Response	Comments
Sing "Jesus Loves Me."	The student sings along, says or mouths some of the words, or otherwise shows familiarity with it.	
Sing "Jesus Loves Me," or some other well-known children's song.	The student sings along, says or mouths some of the words, or otherwise shows familiarity with it.	

Question/Task	Desired Response	Comments
Show the picture of Jesus and the children. Say, "Most people are happy when they are with someone they love. "Who are these children with?"	Jesus.	
"Why are they happy?"	They are with Jesus.	
Show a picture of the devil and ask the following questions:		
"Who is this?"	The devil, Satan.	
"Where does he live?"	Hell or "down there."	
"Where do angels live?"	With God, in Heaven, or similar answer.	
"Where do good people go When they die?"	Heaven or "up there."	
"Where do bad people go?"	Hell or "down there."	
Show the pictures of the boys fighting and the boys shaking hands.		
"Which is the good thing to do?"	Being friendly or shaking hands.	
"Which boys have happy faces?"	The boys being friendly.	
Open a Bible between the two testaments.		
"What are the names of the two parts of the Bible?"	Old Testament and New Testament.	
If no response, say, "These are called testaments. What kinds of testaments are they?"	First part is the Old Testament. Second part is the New Testament.	
If no response, ask, "Which comes first the Old or New Testament?"	Old Testament.	

SECTION TWO:
God

Question/Task	Desired Response	Comments
"Where does God live, in the sky or the ground?"	In the sky.	
"Did God make me?"	Yes.	
"Did He make clouds?"	Yes.	
"Did He make worms?"	Yes.	
"Does God listen to you?"	Yes.	

SECTION THREE:
Jesus

Materials: Pictures or figures dressed like the good Samaritan, a priest, and a Levite, and three other sets of pictures:
1 A bedroom, hospital, and manger
2 A mother and father, mother and son, pair of children, and a father and son
3 Jesus as a boy, a child playing, a child working, a child being destructive

Question/Task	Desired Response	Comments
Show pictures of a bedroom, hospital, and manger. Ask, "Where did Mary put the baby Jesus?"	In a manger.	
Show a picture of a mother and father, a mother and son, a pair of children, and a father and son. Ask, "Which picture is like God and Jesus?"	The father and son.	
"A new boy moved into town. No one wants to play with him. How would Jesus treat the new boy?"	Jesus would be kind to him.	
With figures dressed like the characters, tell the story of the good Samaritan. Ask, "Which of the men would make Jesus happy?" "How should we act toward other people who need help?"	The good Samaritan. Help them, be good to them.	

Question/Task	Desired Response	Comments
Show pictures of Jesus as a boy. Tell that Jesus helped Joseph in the carpenter shop and played with other children. Show pictures of a child playing, a child working, and a child being destructive. Ask,		
"Which would Jesus not act like?"	Jesus would not act like the child who is breaking things.	
"Does Jesus want us to say and do bad things?"	No.	

SECTION FOUR:
The Bible

Materials: Four books
1 Telephone directory
2 Story book
3 Bible
4 Cookbook

Question/Task	Desired Response	Comments
Show the four books. Ask,		
"Which book is best?"	The Bible.	
"Why?"	Because it is God's Word; Because God gave it to us; (or a similar answer).	
Who gave us the Bible—Teacher, Mommy, Daddy or God?	God.	

SECTION FIVE:
The Church

Materials: Six pictures:
1 Church building
2 House
3 Girl praying
4 Boy taking Communion
5 Boy playing ball
6 Girl singing

Question/Task	Desired Response	Comments
Show a picture of a church building and a house. Ask,		
"Where do we usually go to worship with other people?"	The church building.	

Question/Task	Desired Response	Comments
Show pictures of a girl praying, boy taking Communion, a boy playing ball, a girl singing. Ask, "Which do we do in church?"	All but play ball.	
Which day do we go to church; Tuesday, Sunday or Monday?	Sunday.	

SECTION SIX:
Christian Activities

Materials: Some coins and three pictures:
1 Woman talking on a telephone
2 A thief
3 A person praying

Question/Task	Desired Response	Comments
Show a picture of person praying and lady talking on the telephone. Ask, "How is praying like talking?"	We talk to God by praying. The lady talks to someone else by talking on the telephone.	
Show the coins. Ask, "If a person gave you this money, would you keep it or give it to someone who really needs it?"	Give it to someone who needs it.	
"If you found money on a table and knew whose it was, what would you do?"	Give it to the owner.	
Show a picture of a thief and a picture of someone praying. Ask, "Which one is doing wrong?"	The thief.	
"Jesus is God's son, and He died. Why did He die?"	To pay for our sins.	
"If you saw a friend fall off his bicycle, what would you do?"	Help him.	

CONCLUSIONS

Concepts the child needs to understand

1 _____

2 _____

3 _____

4 _____

5 _____

Other Comments

_____

_____

_____

Dates the test was administered	First time	Retests
Section One		
Section Two		
Section Three		
Section Four		
Section Five		
Section Six		

The Spiritual Needs of People With Disabilities

Are the spiritual needs of children with disabilities the same as their age-mates who do not have disabilities? The answer is yes and no. Yes, from the standpoint that everyone needs to have a foundation in the basics of faith:

▼ We need to know the truths in the Bible.
▼ We need to experience salvation.
▼ We need to have a relationship with God and His Son.
▼ We need fellowship in a community of faith.
▼ We need to know that we are uniquely created and have a unique purpose.
▼ We need to be accountable.
▼ Our lives need to demonstrate the fruit of the Spirit.
▼ We need to pray.
▼ We need to serve.

The answer is no for a couple of reasons. First, if the student has cognitive disabilities that prevent him from learning, then his embracing faith will be determined by his mental age. Second, the fact that the student is dealing with why he has a disability may shape his concept of God. There might be a delay in his understanding of God's grace and mercy. At one time I would not have added this second answer for no. Hearing the responses of persons with disabilities over the years has altered my thinking. One man's answer to my question during a seminar helped me reach this conclusion.

The group had done a thorough discussion of the spiritual awareness of people with disabilities and concluded that the person's mental age was the all-important factor in arriving at his spiritual needs. We were about ready to move on, when a man with a serious physical disability asked to speak. He said simply, "All of my life I have asked why I was born this way. The answer has been slow and hard in coming. I am just glad that, in the meantime, I honor God with my disability and don't blame Him."

Helping a student work through his feelings about his disability is a vital role for the church worker.

STEP NINE:
Interview Family

When the student comes to your program, interview the family. The form on pages 199 and 200 is only a sample; make it meet your specific needs. Add any questions you need to get a good overview of how the child functions. Remember to get the information you need to make his placement in the classroom a positive one for him.

PARENT/GUARDIAN INTERVIEW FORM

Name of Student_____ Birthday _____

Address_____City_____State_____Zip_____

Telephone_____ E-mail_____

Names of parents_____

Names of siblings_____

Education

Specific diagnosis _____

Is child in school? Y____N____ Where?_____

Type of placement _____

Teacher_____ Phone_____ E-mail_____

Behavior

Is the child on medication? Y____N____ How often does it have to be administered?_____

Describe the child's behavior. (Is he aggressive? Does he hit, bite, throw, run away, yell, pull hair;

is he self-abusive?)_____

_____

_____

What do you do to control his behavior?_____

_____

How does he deal with people he doesn't know? _____

Food

What are his eating habits? _____

_____

Is he allergic to any foods? _____

Describe his allergic reaction: _____

_____

Are there food restrictions? _____

What do you give him for snacks? _____

Independence

Does he take care of his elimination needs? Y_____ N_____

Does he feed himself? Y_____ N_____

Does he dress himself? Y_____ N_____

Communication

Is his speech understandable to people who don't know him? Y_____ N_____

How does he communicate his basic needs? _____

Ask for a drink? _____

Ask to use the toilet? _____

Does he use any sign language? Y_____ N_____

Does he use a language board? Y_____ N_____

Prosthetic Devices

Does he use a hearing aid? Y_____ N_____ Cane? Y_____ N_____

Wheelchair? Y_____ N_____ Walker? Y_____ N_____ Artificial limbs? Y_____ N_____

Any other prosthetic device? Y_____ N_____

What special care needs should we be aware of? _____

_____

Religious

What have been his previous experiences with going to church? _____

_____

_____

What is the family's religious background and practice? _____

_____

What concepts does he understand? God, Jesus, church, Heaven _____

_____

_____

_____

STEP TEN:
Prepare the Individualized Christian Education Plan

To start the process, organize a team to develop the plan. Include the minister or his designee, a member of the Christian education committee, the children's minister or youth minister (depending on the age of the child), the parents, and the parents of a child without a disability. This group will provide a broad range of insights into the child's spiritual needs. The parents of a child without a disability can communicate to parents of other children that there will be enough staff to go around, and that the teacher can provide equal time to the children who do not have disabilities.

To continue the process, obtain copies of the three documents used in the education of children with disabilities, the IEP (Individualized Education Program) the IFSP (Individualized Family Service Plan), and the Transition Plan. All three have excellent components that can be used by the Christian educator. The school system's IEP gives the student's present level of function, the long-term goals, and the short-term goals. The IFSP, required for the preschool child, details the family's involvement in the learning process of their child. The Transition Plan assists in including the student in the community. The parents will have copies. Reviewing them will help in your own planning.

With this information, the results of the family interview, and the results of the religious awareness test, assemble the team and complete the Individualized Christian Education Plan (ICEP). After completing the form, determine when the child's progress will be assessed. On that date, use the evaluation form for the ICEP (page 206) and set new ICEP goals. Dual purposes will be achieved: the family and staff will know how well the child is doing, and new goals will be modified or added. Always determine when the next evaluation will be done.

Instructions for completing the ICEP

Identifying information:
Name: Note the name the person prefers.
Age: Record the birth date as well.
Parents/Guardians: make guardian relationships clear.

Assesment information:
Present level of religious awareness: Describe where the person is now. Enter notations like "Has never attended Sunday school," "Understands right from wrong," "Is a Christian."

Learner's community activities: "Participates in Special Olympics." "Never goes anywhere without his parents." "Likes to go to the zoo."

Learner's strengths and limitations: "Loves people." "Likes to help people." "Lacks common sense." "Has no fears." "Doesn't read." "Directions must be given one step at a time."

Learner's family involvement in the Christian education of their child: "Want their child to become a Christian." "See the child's involvement as a social outlet." In their own Christian education: "Attend Sunday school faithfully." "Do not attend Sunday school."

Goals

Long-term goal 1: "Joe will learn that God created the world."
▼ Short-term goal 1a: "He will learn that God made day and night."
▼ Short-term goal 1b: "He will learn that God made animals."

Every long-term goal should have several short-term goals. Each goal is planned to help meet the long-term goal. Use additional sheets if necessary. Record the person responsible for the goal and the date of implementation. As the ICEP is used it will be a valuable resource guiding the instruction for the student. It is meant to be a blessing, not a burden.

Methods for including the child in the community and church: "Joe will visit the zoo and have lunch with the class." "He will take tray favors to a children's hospital." "He will spend a night at the church camp." Be sure to include the dates of the events.

In planning for the child's program of spiritual development, it is important to consider where his place of service in the church will be. The ministry the church offers to people with disabilities should not be "what we do with them." Equally important is "what they do with us."
▼ Sing in the musicals.
▼ Participate in other productions.
▼ Serve as greeters and ushers.
▼ Do volunteer work in the church office.
▼ Visit a nursing home.

The list can be almost the same as for any other student in the congregation. Serving is a part of being creative. In my church the lady who directs the children's choirs is a why-didn't-I-think-about-that kind of person. When a child who has serious vision problems had difficulty doing the choreography, the director arranged for her to hold the signs that gave the names of the scenes. She sat in a chair to sing and do her part. The child with the disability can be accommodated and made to be a useful young servant.

Signatures: Each member of the Inclusion Team should sign and date the ICEP.

After completing the ICEP form, explain to the family the **Accident Report Form** (on page 209) and the **Behavior Modification Form** (on page 210). Both will let the parents know that you are seriously interested in ministering to their child and are concerned about his safety.

INDIVIDUALIZED CHRISTIAN EDUCATION PLAN

IDENTIFYING INFORMATION

Learner's name_____

Diagnosis_____Age_____Date of Birth_____

Parents/Guardians_____

Address_____

Area code/telephone _____

E-mail address _____

Placement in public school _____

Name of teacher _____

Address _____

Telephone _____

E-mail address _____

ASSESSMENT INFORMATION

Learner's present level of religious awareness and spritual development:
_____
_____
_____
_____

Learner's present involvment in community activities:
_____
_____
_____
_____

Learner's strengths and limitations:
_____
_____
_____
_____

LEARNER'S FAMILY INVOLVEMENT

In the Christian education of their child:

_____
_____
_____
_____

In their own Christian education:

_____
_____
_____
_____

Is the family open to doing home activities to augment the lesson?

_____
_____
_____
_____

LONG-TERM GOALS

	Description	Parent(s) Responsible	Date of Implementation
1			
2			
3			

SHORT-TERM GOALS

1a			
1b			
2a			
2b			
3a			
3b			

METHODS FOR INCLUSION IN THE COMMUNITY

_____

_____

_____

_____

SIGNATURES

_____

Minister   Date

_____

Christian education staff   Date

_____

Parent(s) representing children without disabilities   Date

_____

Parents of learner   Date

_____

Teacher   Date

_____

Date goals will be evaluated

EVALUATION FORM FOR THE ICEP

(Attach this form to the Individualized Christian Education Plan)

Learner's Name   Date of Evaluation

GENERAL PROGRESS

Area	Strengths	Limitations
Behavior		
Communication		
Learning		
Community Development		
Spiritual Development		

PROGRESS TOWARD LONG-TERM GOALS

Description	Parent(s) Responsible	Date of Implementation
1		
2		
3		

SHORT-TERM GOALS

1a		
1b		
2a		
2b		
3a		
3b		

GENERAL PROGRESS

STATUS OF COMMUNITY INVOLVEMENT

_____

_____

NEW PLANS

_____

_____

LONG TERM GOALS

Description	Responsible Person(s)	Date of Implementation
1		
2		

SHORT TERM GOALS

Description	Responsible Person(s)	Date of Implementation
1a		
1b		
2a		
2b		

SIGNATURES

Minister	date
Christian education staff	date
Parent(s) representing children without disabilities	date
Parents of learner	date
Teacher	date

ACCIDENT REPORT FORM

Note: Please fill out two copies of this and give one to the parents and one to the church secretary.

Date _____ Time _____

To the parent(s) or guardian of _____

During class today, your child acquired the following injury_____

while (what activity led to the injury)_____

_____

_____

_____

_____

The following treatment was applied

Latex gloves used

Ice pack

First aid kit: Band-Aids, first aid cream, burn cream, antiseptic wipes

Other _____

The following people were contacted

Children's ministry coordinator/director

Parent(s) or guardian

911 (for serious accidents only)

Additional comments _____

_____

_____

Please contact me if you have any questions.

_____   _____

Classroom teacher   phone number

_____   _____

Accident witness   phone number

BEHAVIOR MODIFICATION FORM

First Name _____ Last Name _____

Address: _____

City _____ State _____ Zip _____

Parents can be found: *(Please circle one)*

First worship service

Second worship service

Name of Sunday school class _____

Behavior concerns: Please share with us any behaviors we should be aware of such as biting, scratching, or aggressiveness.

_____

_____

_____

_____

_____

Behavior modification plan: Please explain in detail the behavior management plan being used at home and at school to modify any inappropriate behavior that may be exhibited. Our goal is to maintain consistency in the implementation of this plan and to work with you in this process.

_____

_____

_____

_____

_____

STEP ELEVEN:
Anticipate the Future

Because children with disabilities become adults with disabilities, plan to continue providing spiritual nurture for them as teenagers and adults. Generally speaking, most churches do a good job including children with disabilities, a poor job with their teenage counterparts, and go back to doing a good job with adults. As children, the main factor is the difference in development, but the problem at the teenage level is social. If adults are made a part of the congregation, but have an educational experience at their own level, the process works better.

Some suggestions:
▼ Include youth pastors in your planning committee.
▼ Make teenagers in the congregation aware of the needs of their peers who have disabilities.
▼ Ask the minister of adult education to be a part of your planning for the future.

STEP TWELVE:
Enjoy knowing that you are making an eternal difference

Can a person with a disability embrace faith? Become a Christian? Be baptized? Become a member of the church? Whatever language is used, the answer to this important question is the same: Yes!

Students with mental retardation will have the most difficulty with religious concepts. Of this group, 85 percent can be taught the facts about faith on a twelve-year-old level. Being a part of Christian education settings—where matters of faith are presented and the child is exposed repeatedly and consistently to the love of Jesus—will insure the child's understanding of the elements of faith.

In cases where the person's level of function is so low that he simply cannot comprehend basic facts, God understands. As in all situations, the person is surrounded by God's love and mercy. But in situations where the mental age is sufficient to learn, the child should be taught, and brought to faith in Jesus.

Two Exceptional Life Stories

Following the funeral of her son, a mother helped me solidify my belief about the acceptance of Jesus by persons with cognitive disabilities. Her son's autism and serious behavior problems made it difficult to judge his responses to things spiritual. Because his father was a minister, he had been exposed to the church all his life. He had never been baptized. In discussing that, his mother said, "All of us are under God's love, some of us are under His grace. My son was under His grace." If we are faithful in teaching faith, the response is under God's grace.

A favorite memory of mine will always be Helen's baptism. She was a part of a demonstration Sunday school/church program at Johnson Bible College. The teacher assigned to her was a wonder. She drew pictures to illustrate the major parts of our Lord's life and ministry. The gospel lessons found a place in Helen's heart, which had not been affected by the cerebral palsy she had had from birth. After a few lessons, Helen told her teacher she wanted to become a Christian. Wanting to be sure Helen understood the concept, the teacher requested that I talk with her. I asked her why she wanted to be baptized. In labored speech, Helen responded, "Be like Jesus." She became one of the most vibrant Christians I have ever known. She enriched the lives of people around her. Her life was not one of disability, but one of ability. She was not a victim of cerebral palsy; she was a victorious human being. Her life was evidence that her soul had been rehabilitated by the salvation made possible by Jesus, God's Son.

Helen died unexpectedly of pneumonia. A few days after her burial, her mother gave me the set of pictures her teacher had drawn to explain God's plan for rehabilitating the soul. As I looked through the pictures and the lesson plans, I rejoiced that the goals had been met. Helen's wheelchair and communication devices were no longer needed. Her soul, freed from her flawed body, had returned to its Creator.

CHAPTER 18

MINISTERING WITH THE FAMILY
of the Student With a Disability

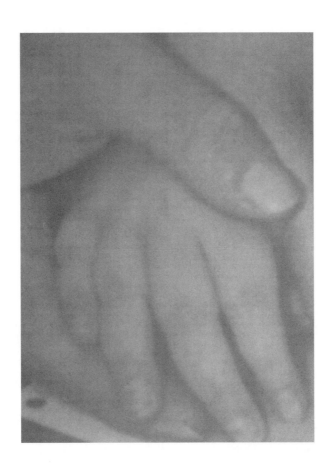

The family of a child with a disability needs the ministry of the church. This ministry starts with understanding. Understand that the family is forever changed, that they question why this happened, that they often deal with a negative, staring society, that educational services are not always easy to get, that their other children have difficulty with the disability, that the information they get is not always clear, that disability is expensive, that the medical community can be confusing, and that their friends often leave. The key is understanding.

Following Jesus' example

Jesus was sensitive to the family of the person with a disability. Jesus healed a boy with epilepsy after His disciples couldn't (Mark 9:18-24). Following a stern discussion with His disciples about their inability to minister to the boy, Jesus radiated a warm concern for his parents. He asked, "How long has he been like this?" Jesus' question is exemplary. Expressing interest in the child and his family is better than a stare or a turned head.

Sometimes parents are blamed for the disability of a child. Such an approach did not originate with Jesus. After meeting a man who was born blind, Jesus' disciples revealed that they had judgmental thoughts (John 9:1-3). Their exchange and Jesus' response provide an eternal answer to the reason for a disability. The man's condition was not due to either his sin or that of his parents. His blindness happened, Jesus said, "So that the work of God might be displayed in his life" (John 9:3). There is no reason to blame, but every reason to support the family, and to help display God's mercy, kindness, love, and hope in their lives and the life of the child.

Families ask questions

"Why did God allow this to happen?" "Is it permanent?" "Can I afford the care?" "Can my child still be productive?" "How do I discipline my child who has a disability?" "Will I still have a normal family life?" "What do I say to people who stare at my daughter and make thoughtless remarks?" "Where do I get more information?" "How do I respond to, 'If you had more faith, God would heal your child'?" "Will my child ever be able to accept Jesus?" "I thought parents naturally loved their children, but I don't feel that way about my son; what's wrong with me?" "What will happen to my child after we are gone?"

These are tough questions. Seeing them in print should give some insight into the needs of these families, their reactions, and their feelings. First Peter 3:15 tells us, "Always be prepared to give an answer to everyone who asks you to give the reason for the hope that you have. But do this with gentleness and respect." Was ever a Bible verse more applicable to a situation? You can, you *must* be prepared to share your reason for hope with the family who has just received a devastating medical diagnosis. You must be prepared to welcome that family visiting your congregation, searching for someone to accept them and their severely disabled child. What will you say when the father or mother in your Bible study group cries out in anguish? Will you offer some pat cliché that does more harm than good, or will you have a well-thought-out, sensitive response? You can be prepared with helpful information about available services; you can be prepared to share the hope we have in Christ; you can be prepared with open arms, a listening ear, and a shoulder to cry on. And remember Peter's admonition: whatever you say, say with gentleness and respect.

Saying the right words

In my experience of working with parents of children with disabilities, I have heard consistent reports about the insensitive, unkind statements people make. They range from, "What do you think God is punishing you for?" to "God knew what He was doing when He selected a strong person like you to have a child like this."

Learn words that will encourage. These examples will help you phrase sentences that will encourage:
▼ "I have learned so much from you as I've watched you handle your child."
▼ "You are the expert on the needs of your child."
▼ "Take care of yourself."
▼ "I see a lot of love in you."
▼ "It is not your fault."

Suggestions from two parents

Drew Mentzer, the father of an adult daughter who has neurofibromatosis and is blind, was the featured speaker for a disability awareness program that I attended. He based his comments on the different feelings of James's family when Herod put James to death, compared with those of Peter's family when Peter was released from prison (Acts 12:1-17). James's family was having a funeral; Peter's family was having a party. Drew's analogy was clear; James's family would be the one with a child with a disability and Peter's family would be the one whose child does not have a disability. Drew's bright mind and sensitive heart are in his suggestions given here.

Billie's developmental delay does not affect her ability to greet others in her Sunday school class. A resident in the independent living program, she gladly serves in this capacity.

▼ Be a servant to the family. Take up the towel and basin. Do not see yourself as superior. The family needs friends who will serve.

▼ See life from their perspective. Learn their vocabulary. Know the world of dealing with a child with a disability.

▼ Encourage the family. They know pain, fear, worry, and grief. Help them know compassion, joy, and hope.

▼ Be sensitive. Don't thank God for your healthy child if your gratitude is based on comparison with their child. Parents of children with disabilities are thankful for them, too. God made us all.

▼ Don't assign blame or ask if they know what they did to cause the problem. Parents suffer from such insensitive questions. I was once asked, "Was it something you did or was it Satan's doing?" God is in charge and does all things according to His purpose and plan for us.

▼ You don't have to be able to provide answers, but be ready to help the family learn good lessons.

▼ Guide families to know that it is all right to ask for help.

▼ Cheer the family on to victory. Be there in the good times and the bad.

▼ Include the family in the life of the congregation. Make it easy for the parents to attend church functions. If their Bible school class is having a party, volunteer to sit with the child.

Drew had a final comment for the entire church; "Minister to both families" were his exact words. A minister by profession, this father of a daughter with a disability was unselfishly reminding us that both families, those without disabilities as well as those with, need to receive and give ministry. Drew's comment suggests that while everyone needs to be ministered to, families dealing with disabilities also need to reach out and minister to others in spite of their situation.

Mary Klentzman is the mother of Jonathan, who at birth sustained severe neurological damage. For the first seven years of his life, he required constant care. She offers eighteen practical suggestions for helping the family.

1 Pray—and let the family know you are praying. Of course, this is the most important thing you can do. Not long ago, a local church was planning a prayer vigil and called to obtain specific prayer needs concerning Jonathan. It was an incredible faith-builder and encouragement for all of us to see God answer the prayers of these precious people.

2 Assure family members by a friendly, reassuring smile or comment that the odd things some of these children do, such as making loud, guttural sounds, are just fine—even joyful at times. This will do wonders to ease any embarrassment they are experiencing.

3 Try to overcome fear of interacting with the child. Ask the parent what the child likes—some like their heads and hands rubbed, others hate it. Don't be afraid to ask—then do it. Many of these kids are not physically fragile.

4 A brief phone call to say you're praying for them is such a blessing. A lot of

these mothers have no adult conversation.

5 Don't criticize the family for decisions they make with their children. People need to understand that no one knows the child as well as his parents. They also need to be aware that these parents face criticism and pressure from therapists, doctors, teachers, and social workers to do more or different things with their child than may be humanly possible. Christians must realize there are factors involved that they really cannot understand because they are not living with this child all the time.

6 Let the parents talk and vent their frustrations. Their trials are of such long duration that the parents don't want to burden others with their constant difficulties, but, occasionally, just talking to someone is very helpful.

7 Be sensitive even when the disability isn't very bad. It is still a loss that can bring a great deal of sadness and uncertainty about the child's future. (I was surprised when the discovery of a relatively mild cerebral palsy in my sixth child, Andrew, brought such pain, especially since I could compare him with Jonathan, the severely and profoundly handicapped fifth child.)

8 Don't be critical when the parents are going through the normal stages of grieving—anger, denial, guilt, etc. People get so concerned about parents being in denial that they don't realize that sometimes this is a needed emotional cushion to survive and bide time until adjustment to their situation and acceptance of the disabilities can be attained. Even then, periodically we grieve again as we discover another problem or delay in development. Be patient and understanding during these difficult times.

9 Dads especially need support from other men. Statistics show that it is even harder for a father to handle a child's disability than it is for moms. Dads would benefit greatly from the prayer support of other men, and from their encouragement and sensitively presented ideas on how they can better interact and play with their children.

10 Most families have a difficult time finding a church where they can feel comfortable worshiping God and gaining fellowship with other believers. Some churches provide Sunday school classes for children with special needs. In ours, precious hosts are prepared to take visiting children or newcomers to their age-appropriate classes and help train the teachers to include and care for them within the classroom. Sadly, we have heard from quite a few families with children with disabilities about their dilemma of not being able to find a church that is sensitive to their circumstances. At some churches these families meet tragic rejection because of their children's special needs rather than the warm acceptance Jesus intends—no matter how different a person appears or behaves. Many opt not to attend anywhere.

11 In one congregation, a special education major from a local university offered to take care of our Jonathan during choir practice on Wednesday nights and Sunday mornings during worship so I could have this wonderful outlet. It wouldn't take much effort if several people volunteered, or even if the church sought out and paid a student to do things like this.

12 Share encouraging Scriptures and tapes (music and sermons) with the parents. Right after Jonathan was born, I listened over and over to a Larnelle Harris tape on God's faithfulness. Each time, Larnelle directed my heart and perspective to a loving Father, building my faith, peace, and joy.

13 Offer to go to the doctor with the parent and child. Pray with them about these appointments and meetings with school personnel. The doctor and school visits can provide some of the worst sources of discouragement and despair for parents. Another suggestion is to offer to care for the parents' other children while they take their child with a disability to the doctor or therapist. Managing to maneuver a wheelchair and other small children can be very difficult. And having the distractions of other children in the room can make it impossible to grasp the information a doctor is relating.

14 Many of these children spend much time in the hospital. You can be a great help by offering to stay with the child at the hospital while Mom goes home to rest and spend time with her other children who desperately need her attention and assurance, too.

15 People who are able can offer to build or repair equipment for the child. This could be as simple as making a wooden bench on which to do therapies. Someone with minimal sewing skills can offer to make attractive bibs for children who drool so much that without bibs their clothes have to be changed frequently during each day.

16 Offer to baby-sit the child while the parents go out on a date. Most of these children are not medically fragile, so anyone can learn to care for them. If the child is fragile, a church can offer to pay a qualified person to stay with the child. Even if it takes a little extra effort to learn what is needed, do it. It is very difficult for most of these parents ever to get away even for an evening

©Standard Publishing

The family of a child with a disability

needs the ministry of the church.

together because they know no one they can ask to take care of their special child. A child's disability puts an incredible strain on a marriage.

17 Offer to stay up all night with the child. You have time to recover. Some parents go years without a decent night's sleep. These parents would be enormously blessed if several people rotated nights with the child. Offer to let the parents go away for the night—perhaps even pay for their hotel bill.

18 Not many people realize the financial constraints put upon parents with physically challenged children. Many times Medicaid is the only medical insurance they can get. To qualify for Medicaid a family usually must meet almost poverty-level income restrictions. Thus, they cannot seek that higher-paying job or bonus, for they will lose the only coverage their child has for the incredibly expensive medical care needed. Thus, a financial strain is placed on the family. Christians could help them with groceries or prepared meals or an occasional love offering. In my case, some families joined together and offered a certain amount of money to pay for any kind of help I desired—nursing or house-cleaning for example. As a result, a team of cleaning professionals came and cleaned our house like it had never been cleaned. That did more to encourage me and lift my load than just about anything, since the regular daily needs of my family make it impossible to clean adequately. The funds provided a weekly service for several months. Praise the Lord!

Helping during four difficult times

There are four times of universal concern for the family. Being aware of these times will enable you to know when to be especially available. Don't withdraw at these times. Send a card. Send an e-mail message. Visit, and find out how things are going. Be there for them!

▼ First, when the diagnosis is made
▼ Second, when the child starts to school
▼ Third, when the child is finished with school
▼ Fourth, when the parents realize they can no longer provide care for their child

Christian education

Providing Sunday school and worship experiences for the child is a must for the family. Christian parents want their child to develop faith, become a Christian, have Christian friends, and grow spiritually.

While serving as an advocate for a family in a multidisciplinary team meeting (M-team, defined on page 226), the principal asked the parents what they wanted more than anything else for their son. The principal was asking for the sake of a goal for the Individual Education Program. The father's response brought the room to reality. He answered, "I want my son to know who Jesus is." Help families meet that eternally important goal.

Respite care is the family's greatest need

A congregation can be a real resource for the family. The family's number-one need is respite care. Simply stated, they need some time away, some extra hands occasionally, and someone to do the chores when time gets tight. Putting yourself in the family's place will allow you to add chores to this list of what will make their days easier.

▼   Transportation to the doctor's office
▼   Shop for the weekly food
▼   Mow the lawn
▼   Do the laundry
▼   Take the siblings to a movie

Why don't all families receive respite care? Oddly enough, the answer is not always, "Because no one has offered." Some families develop defensive attitudes because of the enormous strain they are under, or they may be confused about the help that is available. If you are aware of the reasons the family doesn't get respite care, or may not respond well to an offer of help, you will be in a better position to help them.

▼ The parents develop a martyr complex. "This is my problem. I'll deal with it myself."
▼ They confuse respite care with hospice, thinking, "My child is not sick enough to need that kind of care."
▼ Pride. "I don't need anyone's help."
▼ They have no knowledge of how to obtain available services.
▼ They don't think good care is provided.
▼ Lack of services. Sometimes the services are not available. Other times there is such a long waiting list, the parents simply cannot get help.

Five benefits of respite care

Relaxation—Disability creates a lot of stress; respite care provides opportunities for families to relax and enjoy themselves in order to provide better care for their loved ones.

Enjoyment—Respite care provides time for families to enjoy themselves and pursue activities and interests outside the family.

Stability—Respite care promotes stability by providing a network of support to turn to in times of crisis.

Preservation—Respite care offers families a break from the daily stress that comes with having a family member with a disability. It helps preserve the family unit by warding off potential burnout and marriage and family problems.

Involvement—Respite care offers families an opportunity to participate in activities they otherwise could not. They will not feel isolated.

Two kinds of respite care

▼ Informal—usually provided by family, friends, or church for short periods of time as needed.

▼ Formal—specific programs performed and operated by professionals. Most states offer a respite care program. Help the family find out what is available and if they qualify.

How to begin a respite care program

▼ Discover the need in your church and your community. Find out the number of families and types of services they will need. (See the survey forms on pages 174 and 199.)

▼ Find volunteers. You will need to find responsible people who are willing to be trained. They should have caring hearts and want to support the family. Avoid asking people who are overly committed.

▼ Call a facility that provides respite care and ask for ideas for what is needed in the community and for assistance with training your volunteers.

▼ Offer a training program in which you explain to volunteers what will be required of them. Use a contract that specifies the time, the task, and other requirements to add to the commitment level.

▼ Once you have a list of volunteers, decide what types of programs you will offer and the number of people who will attend each program. If you have a long list of people needing services, you may want to have a rotation schedule so that each person can attend one event before someone else gets to attend two.

▼ Plan an activity, advertise it, and carry it out. For example, arrange a game night for people with disabilities at the church. You could advertise that in order to claim their children at the end of the evening, parents will have to provide a receipt showing that they had an evening out!

▼ Meet with volunteers and get feedback on the event. How did it go? What should you do differently?

▼ Stress confidentiality.

The training of volunteers should include the following elements:

▼ Emphasize that the people receiving care have feelings just like everyone else. They can hear all comments and see all facial expressions. Helpers are there to love, not judge or ridicule.

▼ Provide general information about the type of programs your church will offer: time, place, number of people involved, etc.

▼ Teach volunteers how to communicate with people with disabilities and the proper etiquette. (See pages 52 and 118.)

▼ Review basic first aid skills (provide CPR training, if possible).

▼ Share information from families about the children or adults with whom they will be dealing.

▼ Give adequate instructions about specific duties they will be required to perform (diaper-changing, using feeding tubes, accident clean-ups, etc.).

Ideas for church respite care programs

▼ **Mother's Day Out**

Offer one morning a month when mothers can drop off their children while they participate in a group activity such as shopping and lunch out, or run personal errands.

▼ **Father/Child Events**

Plan an activity in which fathers and their children participate in group activities with other fathers and children (forming a network with others experiencing similar circumstances). This also provides mothers with time off to relax or spend time with her other children.

▼ **Weekend Relief**

This type of care probably should be done in the child's home if at all possible. This allows families time to get away for a quick vacation or just to spend time together, something not often done in families in which disability is present.

▼ **Family Retreats**

Provide a weekend away for the whole family. Offer fun activities as well as support-group activities for the whole family. Group people together (parents, siblings, spouses, those with disabilities, etc.) and allow time for them to share common joys and heartaches. Also provide time for the family to sit down together to discuss what they have learned.

▼ **Trade-Off Program**

Pair families and have each trade one day a week or each month where they care for the other's child for the entire day.

▼ **Emergency Care List**

Offer a list of names and phone numbers of church members who have been trained to provide respite care to use in emergency situations. This list can provide families with a sense of comfort knowing that there are several people they can count on.

A special word about dads

Most of the time in school and church situations, the teachers deal with the mother more than the father. Make an effort to include the father in the Christian education process. It will benefit him and his child.

Neil Smartnick, a student of mine in disability ministry and the father of a daughter with autism, developed the acrostic on the next page to help others better understand fathers dealing with disability.

How to help a sibling deal with disability

Siblings of the child with a disability need attention. While the reaction varies, some siblings will overachieve to make up for the child with the disability. Some will resent the time their parents spend with the child with a disability. Some will learn to be empathetic and choose a special education or helping profession. Some will be embarrassed, and some will be jealous of the child.

Forgotten

The tendency is to comfort the mother because she more often expresses her emotions.

Acquiesced

Dads resign themselves to their societal roles, thus driving a wedge that prevents supportive relationships from forming.

Tired

Most of the time fathers are on the go without rest or recognition, but they keep going. They go from work to caring for the child to giving Mom a break, and then back to work—all without any real support.

Hindered

By society's rules and expectations, the fathers cannot and do not feel they can express their true feelings without being labeled weak—so they grin and bear it. Meanwhile, they are falling apart on the inside.

Emotional

Mothers are not the only parents involved. The child is as much the father's as the mother's. Remember, dads have questions and concerns, yet they are less likely to ask for help—it just isn't their role to care, or show emotion. It is bottled up.

Ready

Just ask dads to help, tell them what to do, or ask them how they are feeling. Dads are not going to come to you and admit that they need help, so be willing to prod them (us) a little.

Whatever the case, here are some ways to help.

▼ Be sensitive to issues of timing. When parents are dealing with life-threatening issues surrounding their child with a disability or illness, that is not the best time to bring up issues relating to siblings. Look for a more appropriate time.

▼ Remember that siblings need attention at times of family crises. When medical problems arise and the parents are attending to them, do something for the siblings.

▼ It is important that in your dealings with the siblings you minimize, not maximize, their feelings about the situation. They may feel guilty that they are not disabled. They may feel guilty that they can't provide the help their parents need. When you are with these children you need to be careful that you do not add to these feelings. Convey the idea that you are glad to be with them, that you would be willing to spend time with them even if they didn't have a sibling with a disability. Yours is not a pity mission, it is an act of friendship.

▼ Encourage families to define their roles as family members and stick to them. Do not allow siblings to be seen as other caretakers for their brother or sister.

▼ Encourage parents to share information with their children. In the absence of accurate information, medical terms can be given false meaning in the minds of children—meaning that suggests something much more severe than it really is.

▼ When appropriate, host third-person discussions. They may start with something like this: "I understand that sometimes brothers and sisters of children with disabilities think that the disability or illness is their fault, caused by something they did or said or thought. Do you ever wonder about this?"

▼ Become familiar with the disability or disease so you will be prepared to answer questions you may be asked.

▼ Provide activities for siblings to maximize their self-worth. Mission projects are a great way to do this.

▼ Offer respite care for parents, so that they can spend time with the siblings.

▼ Provide activities designed just for parents and siblings of children with disabilities or illness. Offer respite care during this time.

▼ Offer activities to distract siblings from the daily stress of living with a person with disabilities. Siblings are often unable to attend youth group activities due to lack of transportation and limited family funds. Make these available by offering the sibling a ride or setting up a program within your church that will assist in paying expenses for children whose parents cannot afford to send them to activities or on trips.

▼ Make a list of available resources within your community. Offer this list to families on a regular basis.

▼ Find your local SibShops (workshops for siblings of children with disabilities) and promote them within your congregation. If there is not one nearby, consider allowing one to meet in your building. Encourage singles and seniors to volunteer at the local SibShops.

What can parents do?

▼ Give your children age-appropriate information about their brother or sister's disability or illness.

▼ Communicate openly and honestly about all aspects of family issues.

▼ Involve siblings in the family decision-making process.

▼ Don't give siblings responsibilities beyond their maturity or preparation.

▼ Avoid treating siblings as caretakers for their brother or sister with a disability or illness.

▼ Treat all of your children as equals. Don't give one of them a higher "status" in sibling ranking.

▼ Allow siblings to work out conflicts themselves. It is natural for brothers and sisters to fight.

▼ Allow siblings to express their feelings openly and honestly. Value their opinions.

▼ As much as possible, spend one-on-one time with each of your children.

▼ Involve yourself in outside activities that typical siblings enjoy (i.e., go to ball

games, help lead a Girl Scout troop, etc.).
▼ Use respite care when offered. If not offered, find it.
▼ Spend time alone with your spouse.

The school system

Dealing with the school system can be a frustrating and sometimes frightening experience for parents who are new to the procedures. One of the major stress times in the life of a family dealing with disability is when the child enters school. A church's disability ministry can provide a real service to the family by being aware of and sensitive to this stressful time and provide love, support, encouragement, and information.

Opportunities for service include hosting an Individual Education Program (IEP) workshop (definition below), providing an advocate to attend school meetings with the family, or supporting the family with prayers, cards, and telephone calls. The information about the IEP will give the basics for helping the family. The more experience you gain working with an IEP team, the more comfortable you will be.

A Summary of IDEA

IDEA is an acronym for Individuals With Disabilities Education Act of 1990. It is an update of PL-94-142 of 1975, a federal law that mandates the states to provide free and appropriate education for children with disabilities. It also directs that the education be in the classroom with his typical age-mates if possible, or "in the least restrictive environment" (LRE). Further, IDEA requires that a Multidisciplinary Team (M-Team) convenes and prepares an Individual Education Program (IEP), making sure that the parents are aware of their rights.

Some basic information about these components will help a congregation minister to the family.

The Multidisciplinary Team

The M-Team is made up of the people who are the most interested in the child's appropriate education program.
▼   Parents, legal guardian, or surrogate
▼   The regular classroom teacher
▼   The teacher who will be responsible for carrying out the program
▼   The school principal or his designee
▼   Any specialist, physical, speech or occupational therapist, psychologist, etc.
▼   Anyone else invited by the parent or the school

The purposes of the M-Team are to determine the child's eligibility for special education, create the IEP, make sure the IEP is carried through, and arrange for a Transition Plan.

The Transition Plan is developed by the time the child is fourteen years old. In it, the M-Team outlines the plan for future education, residential care, or a vocation.

The Individualized Education Program (IEP)

The IEP is a legally required document that contains the following components:

▼ A statement of the child's level of educational functioning, both from the special education and regular education standpoint
▼ A statement of the measurable long-term and short-term goals
▼ A statement of all the services and support the child will receive
▼ A statement of the percentage of time the child will spend in regular education
▼ A statement of how the child will be assessed in statewide testing
▼ The date the services will begin, their frequency, and who will be responsible
▼ A statement of how the child's progress will be measured and how the parents will be informed about the progress
▼ The date the child will be reevaluated
▼ Signatures of all participants (The parent's/guardian's signatures and approval of the plan make the IEP valid.)

Parental rights

School systems are required to present the parents their rights in writing. Some of the basic rights include

▼ The parents must be contacted before their child is evaluated or placement is determined.
▼ The child must be tested in his native language.
▼ The parents have the right to have the test results explained to them.
▼ If the parents disagree with the test results, they can have their child retested by someone outside the school system.
▼ The child must be placed in the least restrictive environment (LRE) possible for him to maximize his learning potential.
▼ The school system must contact the parents before changing their child's educational program, destroying their child's records, transferring their child's records to another school, or releasing their child's records to other agencies.
▼ The parents have the right to review/copy all school records pertaining to their child's special education.
▼ The parents can arrange for a surrogate parent if they cannot represent their child.

Other ways the church can help

Provide information.

▼ Help families gather and organize information regarding their child's specific disability.
▼ Attend medical appointments to provide an unbiased and unemotional evaluation of the information presented.

Help locate or begin an appropriate support group.
▼ Offer the use of your facilities for community groups.
▼ Be aware of and utilize existing community support groups.
▼ Be available to the family.

Help the family maintain their church activities.
▼ Provide baby-sitting to allow attendance at church functions.
▼ Don't expect the family to work in the programs for their children.
▼ Be certain all family members are included in the life of the congregation.
▼ Make every effort to keep the family involved in church.

Offer financial assistance.
▼ Ask about the family's financial situation.
▼ Provide camp and retreat scholarships.
▼ Assist in the purchase of special equipment.
▼ Be sure the family is aware and takes advantage of public-funding sources.

Train the entire congregation to assist the family.
▼ Teach young children how to react positively to people with disabilities.
▼ Utilize the energy of youth groups.
▼ Educate adults on disability issues.

The family will be better off because you and the congregation care and want to help. Find out what they need by being close enough to notice. Follow Drew's advice: "Cheer them on to victory. Be there in the good times and the bad."

After reading an advance copy of Exceptional Teaching, *Julie said, "This chapter describes my family and all that we're going through, but I could never verbalize my needs so clearly if asked by someone in our church."*

©Standard Publishing

GOOD DISABILITY MINISTRY PROGRAMS

Name of program: **Disabilities Ministry**
Name of church: **First Evangelical Free Church**
Location: Fullerton, California

Purpose: Our goal is to identify and break down any barriers that keep people with disabilities and their families from being able to fully participate in the body life of this church.

Components: Sunday school classes
- ▼ Children are included in the class with peers if possible.
- ▼ A class for children with disabilities (ages eight to fouteen)
- ▼ A class for young children (ages three to seven) who need one-on-one attention.
- ▼ Fellowship of Friends is designed for people with developmental disabilities to meet together on Sunday morning to share their frustrations, joys, dreams, and faith in Jesus Christ.

Deaf ministry
- ▼ Interpreting for the deaf and hard-of-hearing is provided during one morning service.
- ▼ Transcriptions of the weekly sermon are available by request.
- ▼ Headsets to help amplify the sound in the worship center are available during Sunday services and other events.

Support groups
- ▼ MoKSN stands for Moms of Kids With Special Needs. The group meets every other month and a newsletter is sent to members.
- ▼ MS Support Group meets monthly, except during the summer. The purpose of the group is for people with MS and their spouse or support person to meet for encouragement, information, fellowship, prayer, and fun.

Special events
- ▼ The church has its own Special Olympics team.
- ▼ S.O.S. (Save Our Sanity) is a free respite program for parents who have a child with a disability. Siblings are welcome. The program meets every other month.
- ▼ Friday Night Live is a monthly social event combined with disability ministries from other churches in the community.

Contact: Connie Hutchinson, Director
Address: 2801 North Brea Boulevard
Fullerton, CA 92835-2799
Telephone: 714-529-5544
Fax: 714-255-9437
TTY: 714-257-4362
E-mail: connie@fefcful.org
Web: www.fefcful.org

Name of program: **ACCESS**
Church: **McLean Bible Church**
Location: Vienna, Virginia

Purpose: Providing spiritual accessibility so that all may worship.

Components: Sunday school classes
- Beautiful Blessings are Bible school classes for children with disabilities who need one-on-one attention and are medically fragile. These classes are also available during the summer children's program.
- Beautiful Buddies are provided for students who have mild to moderate disabilities. With this assistance the children are included in their regular Sunday school classes. The buddies are also available for the Sunday evening programs.
- Circle of Friends is designed to facilitate peer friendships between teens with and without a disability during small groups and retreats.
- Friendship Fellowship is an adult Bible study for teens and adults who are developmentally delayed.
- The parents determine the decision about class placement. Children's Ministry values inclusion, and Student Ministries makes every effort to include teenagers wherever possible.

Family support
- Parent-to-Parent meets on the second and fourth Sundays of the month. This support group allows parents of children with special needs to meet other parents who understand the day-to-day struggles faced. Prayer is a vital part of the group. Guest speakers provide information about doctors, IEP meetings, etc.
- Breakaway meets twice a month. It is a respite care program for children with special needs that allows their parents a little "break away."
- Occasional date nights for parents.
- Family activities are held several times each year.
- Family retreat in the summer.
- Summer camp.

Other services
- Special parking
- Accessible facilities
- Sign interpreter available
- Bibles available in large print or on tape at the welcome center
- Resource and lending library
    - Books available that deal with tax information, estate planning, parenting, encouragement, etc.
    - Notebooks with services available in the Metro DC area for people and children with disabilities.
    - Bible on tape for those who have vision impairment.
    - Braille materials available in lobby
- Counseling Center provides professional marriage and family counselors.
- Caring Ministries offer meals for families or individuals in an emergency, as well as small home repairs and improvement.

Contact: Diane Anderson, Director
Address: 8925 Leesburg Pike
Vienna, Virginia 22182
Telephone: 703-790-5590
E-Mail: danderson@mcleanbible.org
Web: www.mcleanbible.org

Name of program:	**With Open Arms**
Church:	**La Croix Church**
Location:	Cape Girardeau, Missouri
Purpose:	We endeavor to make ministry with families experiencing disability a natural part of church life, not a special one.
Components:	Inclusion: All children are included in all children's ministry programs, using shepherds and adapted curriculum where needed to allow maximum participation of all children.
Family support:	Opportunities for parents and siblings to experience full, supportive spiritual growth through:

- ability to worship together;
- small group (Bible study) experience with child care provided, when needed; and
- support resources.

As we grow, we have a vision to provide respite care through

- organized church-based fun activities for the child, and
- occasional in-home care for the child.

Contact:	Kristy Mehner
Address:	3102 Lexington Avenue
	Cape Girardeau, MO 63701
Telephone:	573-339-0302
	kmehner@lacroixchurch.org
	www.lacroixchurch.org

Name of program:	**Remove the Roof Ministry**
Church:	**Woodlawn Christian Church**
Location:	Knoxville, Tennessee
Purpose:	The Disability Ministry of WCC seeks to remove any barrier that would prevent participants from functioning to the full extent of their abilities in the family of faith.
Components:	Inclusion assistants: With the supervision of the children's director, children with disabilities are included in their age-appropriate classes with help for the teacher and assistants.
Self-contained class:	The Soldiers of the Cross Sunday school class is available for adults with developmental disabilities.
Interpreted services:	Sunday school classes and worship services are signed. Amplification devices are available.
Family ministry:	Families who have children with disabilities are served by a plan that links them with a family in the congregation who prays for them, sends cards to them, and in general keeps the Ministry Team informed of special needs that may arise.
Community participation:	Individuals and groups in the church are encouraged to participate in local organizations and ministries serving persons with disabilities.

Contact person: Connie Litts, Office Manager
Address: 4339 Woodlawn Pike
Knoxville, TN 37920
Telephone: 865-573-6721
E-Mail: wcc@woodlawncc.org
Web: www.woodlawncc.org

Name of program: **Special Needs Children's Program**
Church: **Mt. Washington Church of Christ**
Location: Cincinnati, Ohio

Purpose: The MWCC program, in its beginning stage, is designed to include children with disabilities in their regular classes.

Components: Inclusion: Special Needs buddies are provided for children with disabilities age birth to nine.

Parent Support: Encouragement is given to parents as needed.

Contact person: Betty Howell, Children's Minister
Address: 6986 Salem Road
Cincinnati, Ohio 45230
E-mail: bhowell@mtwashcc.com
Telephone: 513-231-9482
Fax: 513-231-6751

Name of Program: **Beyond Limits**
Church: **Crossroads Christian Church**
Location: Corona, California

Purpose: We recognize the value and the needs of each person regardless of his or her physical, mental, or emotional limitations. We strive to offer opportunities for those with disabilities, and their families, to rise to the potential for which God created them. Through our programs, we hope to be a church where anyone can come for acceptance, support, and encouragement.

Components: Christian Education
▼ Mainstreamed Sunday school classes
▼ Adult Bible classes
▼ Mainstreaming buddies for children
▼ Specialized class for children with special needs

Family Support
▼ Parent support group
▼ IEP workshops & other topics

▼ Outreach respite programs
▼ Respite core

General
▼ Transportation (includes wheelchair transportation)
▼ Camp
▼ Sign-language interpretation
▼ Volunteer training
▼ Monthly social activities

Contact Person:	Julie Keith
Address:	2331 Kellogg Avenue
	Corona, California 92881
E-mail:	julie@crossroadschurch.com
Telephone:	909-737-4664
Fax:	909-278-3176

Name of Program:	**Special Needs Ministry**
Church:	**Mountain Christian Church**
Location:	Joppa, Maryland

Purpose: The ministry works to provide meaningful inclusion in the Sunday school and worship for children with disabilities.

Components: Christian Education
▼ Signs of Life is our deaf ministry and includes deaf small groups, fellowship, and social opportunities such as retreats and interpreted services and workshops
▼ Circle of Friends (monthly parent and sibling support group)
▼ Parent Support Class (siblings included)
▼ Chosen and Precious (three nights of camping)
▼ Special Needs 5-Day VBS, seven-year's experience, has grown to serve more than fifty families with children with disabilities. A staff of more than one hundred adults and staff and teenage buddies serve as mentors, leaders, and huggers.

Contact:	Linda and Don Moore
	1824 Mountain Road
	Joppa, MD 21085
E-mail:	lindalivin4jc@hotmail.com
Telephone:	410-877-1824
Fax:	410-877-7141

RESOURCES

Establish your own method of getting materials to learn more about the students you are including in your class. Good materials exist, but because they go out of print, aren't widely marketed, or are privately published, they aren't easy to find. So you will have to extend some effort to develop a practical, easy way to stay abreast of the information you need to include the student in your class.

Find a good bibliography. I use *Dimensions of Faith and Congregational Ministries with Persons with Developmental Disabilities and Their Families.* The latest issue was done in 2000. Order this reference guide from Building Community Supports Project, PO Box 6810, Piscataway, NJ 08855-6810. The work is published by the University Affiliated Program of New Jersey in partnership with the Religious Division of the American Association on Mental Retardation. It contains a lot of helpful materials. Religious education guides and curricula and resources for people with developmental disabilities and their families are two of the several headings.

A Textbook or Two

Staying current with children with disabilities is easy with a copy of *Children With Disabilities.* Edited by Dr. Mark Batshaw, the book is a comprehensive guide to the major disabilities and issues pertaining to children with disabilities. It is available through Paul H. Brookes Publishing Company, PO Box 10624, Baltimore, Maryland 21285-0624. Ask for the latest edition and a catalog. Brookes has excellent publications on disability issues.

A college textbook on special education would be another helpful resource. There are several good ones. A widely used text is *Educating Exceptional Children* by Samuel A. Kirk, James J. Gallaher, and Nicholas J. Anastasiow. Published by Houghton Mifflin, the book is in its ninth edition.

Another excellent one is *Exceptional Lives* by Rud Turnbull, Ann Turnbull, Marilyn Shank, Sean Smith, and Dorothy Leal. Merrill, an imprint of Prentice Hall, publishes it. The third edition was published in 2001.

Textbooks can be expensive. Your public library probably will have a good text on hand. Just be sure it is written after 1995.

Abortion

For more information on the aftereffects of abortion, read Brent Rooney's article, "Is Cerebral Palsy Ever a 'Choice'?" on his web site at www.vcn.bc.ca/~whatsup. You may also want to get on the mailing list for *The Post-Abortion Review* by contacting The Elliot Institute, at PO Box 7348, Springfield, IL 62791, or at www.afterabortion.org. Another article well worth reading on this site is "Impact of Vacuum Aspiration Abortion on Future Childbearing." You may also want to visit the Association for Interdisciplinary Research web site at www.abortionresearch.com.

Suggestions for Bibles

Is there a Bible that is good to use for students who have reading and learning problems? Yes, the three that follow are good.

The Bible for Today's Young Reader, published by Thomas Nelson in 1991, is good for students with cognitive disabilities. Even if the child can't read well or at all, the listening experience is enhanced. Unfortunately this book is out of print.

God's Story: The Bible Told as One Story is paraphrased by Karyn Henley and published by Tyndale House, 1998.

The Young Reader's Bible, 70 Easy-to-Read Bible Stories is a Standard Publishing product of 1998.

Internet

Log on to the net. Entering the diagnosis to do a search will result in a lot of useful information.

A good one is NICHCY. National Information Center for Children and Youth With Disabilities provides fact sheets on many disabilities. They can be written at PO Box 1492, Washington, DC 20013; e-mailed at nichcy@aed.org; telephoned at 1-800-695-0285 (Voice/TTY). The Web is www.nichcy.org.

Organizations

Two of the oldest organizations serving their respective populations are ARC and UCP. Tell them what you are doing and they will provide information.

The Arc (formerly the Association for Retarded Citizens of the United States)
1010 Wayne Avenue, Suite 650
Silver Spring, MD 20910
For publications: www.TheArcPub.com.
301-565-3842.
E-mail: Info@thearc.org.
www.thearc.org.

United Cerebral Palsy Associations, Inc.
1660 L Street NW, Suite 700
Washington, DC 20036
800-872-5827
202-776-0406
E-mail: ucpnatl@ucp.org.
TTY: 202-973-7197
www.ucpnatl@ucp.org

More Organizations

There are scores of organizations that advocate the needs of specific disability groups. These are selected because the disability they represent is mentioned in this book.

American Psychiatric Association
1400 K St. NW
Washington, D.C. 20005
202-682-6220
www.psych.org

American Association on Mental Retardation (AAMR)
(I consistently get good information from this group.)
Religion and Spirituality Division
444 N Capitol Street NW #846
Washington, DC 20001-1512
800-424-3688
Fax: 202-387-2193
www.aamr.org

National Organization for Albinism and Hypopigmentation (NOAH)
PO Box 959
East Hampstead, NH 03826-0959
800-473-2310
603-887-2310 (phone and fax)
www.albinism.org

Angelman Syndrome Foundation
414 Plaza Drive, Suite 209
Westmont, IL 60559
800-IF ANGEL
630-734-9267
www.angelman.org

National Aphasia Association
29 John Street, Suite 1103
New York, NY 10038
800-922-4622
212-267-2814
E-mail: naa@aphasia.org
www.aphasia.org

American Juvenile Arthritis Organization
1314 Spring Street NW
Atlanta, GA 30309
404-872-7100
Fax: 404-872-0457
www.ajao.org

Asthma and Allergy Foundation of America
1233 20th Street NW, Suite 402
Washington, DC 20036
800-7-ASTHMA
Fax: 202-466-8940
E-mail: info@aafa.org
www.aafa.org

National Ataxia Foundation
2600 Fernbrook Lane, Suite 119
Minneapolis, MN 55447
763-553-0020
Fax: 763-553-0167
E-mail: naf@ataxia.org
www.ataxia.org

National Attention Deficit Disorder Association (NADDA)
1788 Second Street, Suite 200
Highland Park, IL 60035
847-432-ADDA
Fax: 847-432-5874
E-mail: mail@add.org
www.add.org

National Autism Hotline/Autism Services Center
605 Ninth Street, Prichard Building
PO Box 507
Huntington, WV 25710-0507

304-525-8014
Fax: 304-525-8026

Birth Defect Research for Children, Inc.
930 Woodcock Road, Suite 225
Orlando, FL 32803
Fax: 407-895-0802
www.birthdefects.org

American Cancer Society
800-ACS-2345
www.cancer.org

The 5p- Society (Cri-du-chat)
PO Box 268
Lakewood, CA 90714-0268
888-970-0777
Fax: 562-920-5240
E-mail: director@fivepminus.org
www.fivepminus.org

Association for Children With Down Syndrome
4 Fern Place
Plainview, NY 11803
516-933-4700
Fax: 516-933-9524
E-mail: info@acds.org
www.acds.org

National Down Syndrome Congress
7000 Peachtree-Dunwoody Road, Suite 100
Atlanta, GA 30328-1655
800-232-NDSC
E-mail: NDSCcenter@aol.com
www.ndsccenter.org

National Down Syndrome Society
666 Broadway, Suite 810
New York, NY 10012
800-221-4602
212-460-9330
Fax: 212-979-2873

Epilepsy Foundation
4351 Garden City Drive
Landover, MD 20785-7223
800-EFA-1000
301-459-3700
www.efa.org

National Fragile X Foundation
PO Box 190488
San Francisco, CA 94119-0488
800-688-8765
510-763-6030
Fax: 510-763-6223
NATLFX@sprintmail.com
www.nfxf.org

National Head Injury Foundation
1776 Massachusetts Avenue NW, Suite 100
Washington, DC 20036-1904
800-444-6443 helpline
202-296-6443

HEAR Now
6700 Washington Avenue S
Eden Prairie, MN 55344
800-648-HEAR (Voice/TDD)
www.sotheworldmayhear.org

Alexander Graham Bell Association for the Deaf
2000 M Street NW, Suite 310
Washington, DC 20036
202-337-5220
TTY: 202-337-5221
Fax: 202-337-8314
www.agbell.org

Laurent Clerc National Deaf Education Center
Gallaudet University
800 Florida Avenue NE
Washington, DC 20002-3695
202-651-5051
Voice/TTY: 202-651-5340
TDD: 202-651-5052
Fax: 202-651-5054
E-mail: clearinghouse.infortogo@gallaudet.edu
www.clerccenter.gallaudet.edu/index.html

American Heart Association National Center
7272 Greenville Avenue
Dallas, TX 75231-4596
214-373-6300
Fax: 214-706-1341
www.americanheart.org
Heart & stroke info: 800-AHA-USA1
ECC info: 877-AHA-4-CPR
Stroke info: 888-4-STROKE
Women's health: 888-MY-HEART

National Kidney Foundation
30 East 33rd Street, Suite 1100
New York, NY 10016
800-622-9010
212-889-2210
Fax: 212-689-9261
E-mail: info@kidney.org
www.kidney.org

Learning Disabilities Association of America
4156 Library Road
Pittsburgh, PA 15234
412-341-1515
412-341-8077
Fax: 412-344-0224

National Center for Learning Disabilities
381 Park Avenue S, Suite 1401
New York, NY 10016
212-545-7510
888-575-7373
Fax: 212-545-9665
www.ld.org

Muscular Dystrophy Association
3300 E Sunrise Drive
Tucson, AZ 85718-3208
800-572-1717
E-mail: mda@mdausa.org
www.mdausa.org

Prader-Willi Syndrome Association
5700 Midnight Pass Road
Sarasota, FL 34242
800-926-4797
941-312-0400
Fax: 941-312-0142
E-mail: pwsausa@aol.com
www.pwsausa.org

International Rett Syndrome Association
9121 Piscataway Road
Clinton, MD 20735
301-856-3334
Fax: 301-856-3336
irsa@rettsyndrome.org
www.rettsyndrome.org

National Association for Sickle Cell Disease, Inc. (NASCD)
3345 Wilshire Boulevard
Los Angeles, CA 90010-1880
800-421-8453
Fax: 213-736-5211

Spina Bifida Association of America
4590 MacArthur Boulevard, NW Suite 250
Washington, DC 20007-4226
800-621-3141
202-944-3285
Fax: 202-944-3295
E-mail: sbaa@sbaa.org
www.sbaa.org

Tourette Syndrome Association
42-40 Bell Boulevard
Bayside, NY 11361-2820
800-237-0717
718-224-2999
Fax: 718-279-9596
E-mail: ts@tsa-usa.org
www.tsa-usa.org

American Council of the Blind
1155 15th Street NW, Suite 1004
Washington, DC 20005

800-424-8666
202-467-5081
www.acb.org

American Foundation for the Blind
15 W 16th Street
New York, NY 10011
800 AFB-LINE
212-620-2147

MINISTRY RESOURCES

There are many faith groups that have consultants in disability ministry, provide materials, and work to include the disability community in the life of the church. This list is not meant to be all-inclusive. Representatives of various faith groups and I selected the entries based on our experience with these organizations.

The Elizabeth M. Boggs Center on Developmental Disabilities
Robert Wood Johnson Medical School
335 George Street, PO Box 2688
New Brunswick, NJ 08903-2688
732-235-9300
Fax: 732-235-9330
E-mail: gaventwi@umdnj.edu
Information on conferences, resource persons from around the country, and membership. Members receive a quarterly division newsletter, and AAMR newsletter and publications.

American Baptist Churches, USA
Educational Ministries
PO Box 851
Valley Forge, PA 19482-0851
800-ABC-3USA, ext. 2411
E-mail: rmcnaney@abc-usa.org
www.abc-usa.org

National Christian Resource Center Bethesda Lutheran Homes & Services, Inc.
(This group provides excellent information.)
700 Hoffman Drive
Watertown, WI 53094
800-369-INFO
E-mail: ncrc@blhs.org
www.blhs.org/outreach/ncrc.html

The Christian Church Foundation for the Handicapped (Church of Christ)
PO Box 9869
Knoxville, TN 37940
865-546-5921
Fax:865-525-2282
E-mail: jimpierson@ccfh.org
www.ccfh.org

Christian Council on Persons With Disabilities
7120 W Dove Court
Milwaukee, WI 53223
414-357-6672
E-mail: info@ccpd.org
www.ccpd.org

The Christian Reformed Church: Committee on Disability Concerns
(They have a useful newsletter.)
2850 Kalamazoo Avenue SE
Grand Rapids, MI 49560
616-246-0801
Fax: 616-224-5895
E-mail: crcna@crcna.org
www.crcna.org/cr/crdc

Church of the Brethren
Association of Brethren Caregivers
1451 Dundee Avenue
Elgin, IL 60120
800-323-8039
847-742-5100, ext. 300
Fax: 847-742-6103
E-mail: abc@brethren.org
www.brethren.org/abc

Church of the Nazarene
6401 The Paseo
Kansas City, MO 64131
816-333-7000, ext. 2330
Fax: 816-363-3100
E-mail: wmvolunteer@nazarene.org
www.nazarene.org

Episcopal Disability Network
3024 East Minnehaha Parkway
Minneapolis, MN 55406
888-422-0320, pin #6634
Fax: 612-722-3690
E-mail: disability99@earthlink.net
www.edn4ministry.org/old_index.html

Evangelical Lutheran Church in America
Division of Social Ministry Organizations
8765 West Higgins Road
Chicago, IL 60631
800-638-3522, ext. 2692
773-380-2700
Fax: 773-380-1465
E-mail: infor@elca.org
www.elca.org

Community Table Minneapolis Area Synod
122 West Franklin Avenue, Suite 600
Minneapolis, MN 55404
612-870-3610
Fax: 612-870-0170
www.mpls-synod.org/index.html

The Healing Community
521 Harrison Avenue
Claremont, CA 91711
909-621-6808
Resources on accessibility, worship, congregational ministry

JAF Ministries
(Write for the location of their regional office.)
PO Box 3333
Agoura Hills, CA 91376
818-707-5664
www.joniandfriends.org

Lutheran Church–Missouri Synod
1333 South Kirkwood
St. Louis, MO 63122-7295
888-THE-LCMS
314-965-9000
Fax: 888-LCMS-FAX
E-mail: infocenter@lcms.org
www.lcms.org
Also contact Bethesda Lutheran Home or
Marlys Taege at Christian Council for Persons
With Disabilities.

Lutheran Special Education Ministries
Ephphatha Center
6861 E Nevada Avenue
Detroit, MI 48234-2983
313-368-1220
Fax: 313-368-0159
www.comnet.org/local/tip/records/013630000.html

MMA (Mennonite Mutual Aid)
Stewardship Education Center
PO Box 483
1110 North Main Street
Goshen, IN 46527
800-348-7468
219-533-9511
Fax: 219-533-5264
E-mail: stewardship@mma-online.org
www.mma-online.org

In Canada:
Mental Health and Disabilities Program
Mennonite Central Committee Canada
134 Plaza Drive
Winnipeg, MB R3T 5K9
204-261-6381
E-mail: canada@mennonitecc.ca
www.mcc.org/canada/health.html

National Organization on Disability, Religion and Disability Program
910 Sixteenth Street NW, Suite 600
Washington, DC 20006
202-293-5960

Fax: 202-293-7999
E-mail: religion@nod.org
www.nod.org

Presbyterian Church (USA)
Social Welfare Organization
100 Witherspoon Street
Louisville, KY 40202-1396
502-569-5000
Fax: 502-569-5018
www.pcusa.org

Reformed Church in America
Office for Education and Faith Development
4500 60th Street SE
Grand Rapids, MI 49512-9670
616-698-7071
E-mail: rcamail@rca.org
www.rca.org

General Conference of Seventh Day Adventists
12501 Old Columbia Pike
Silver Spring, MD 20904-6600
301-680-6000
www.adventist.org

Southern Baptist Convention
901 Commerce Street
Nashville, TN 37203
615-244-2355
www.sbc.net
Special Education Today is a quarterly magazine published by Southern Baptist Sunday School Board for family members and church leaders who meet the special needs of persons with handicaps and disabilities. Includes forum for sharing ideas and success stories, music and recreation ideas, articles written by persons with disabilities, poetry, and resource/church leadership information.

United Church of Christ
United Church Board for Homeland Ministries
700 Prospect Avenue
Cleveland, OH 44115-1100
216-736-3800
Fax: 216-736-3803
E-mail: baylorb@ucc.org
www.ucc.org

United Methodist Church
United Methodist Publishing House, Office of
   Persons with Disabilities
201 8th Avenue South
PO Box 801
Nashville, Tennessee 37202
800-251-8591

INDEX